DA REP
UTE ABLE

VOL 3

TEARS STILL INVINCIBLE

Julius Clark Jones

AF100119

CHAPTERS

Introduction 4

The Beginning 6

Set The Record Straight 13

The Tone Was Definitely Set 19

Back Down Memory Lane 25

Things Come Too A End 32

Hudson County Jail 41

Here Come The Feds 47

Getting Sentence 51

Welcome To Yardville 55

Finally Northern State Prison 63

The Feds Welcome to Otisville 72

Finally Stop Fort Dix Federal Prison 96

Da Journey Is Over Welcome Home 105

Separation Equals Growth 117

A Messages to My Readers 146

INTRODUCTION

From a very young age I knew I was different. There I was, a little boy sneaking in the middle of the night to listen to his mama's conversation. Hearing my mama shed tears again, it did something to me as a child. I vowed to myself it would be the last time. I knew I needed to step up so at age 10 I hit the block. A young in' lion hearted but at the same time still searching for love. Let me take you through a journey about when a man doesn't hold a little black boy's hand and doesn't guide him into becoming a man. A tale of struggle and pain. That little black boy, like so many of us, ends up being a product of his environment....

DA REP UTE ABLE VOL 3

TEARS STILL INVINCIBLE

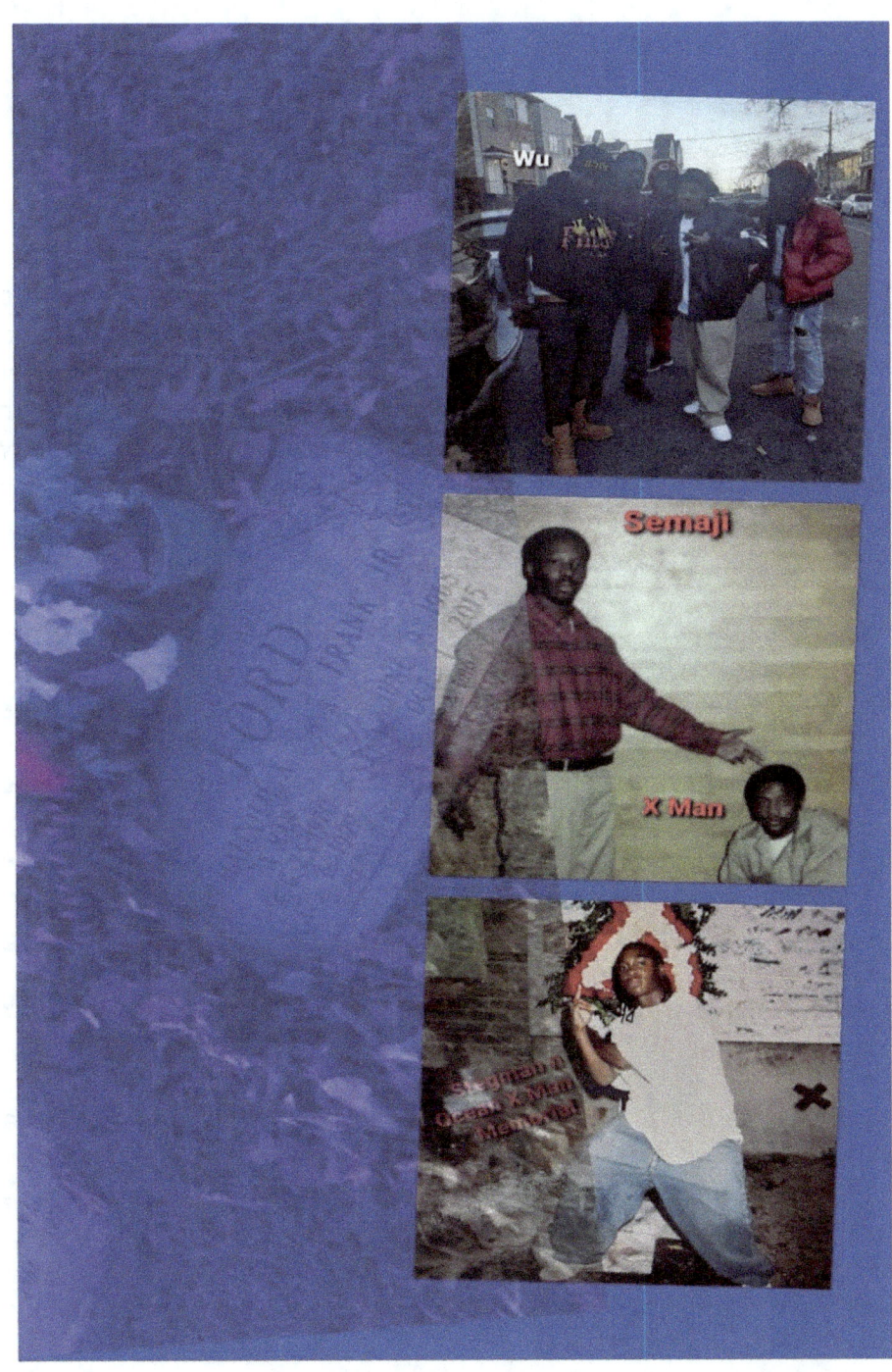

The Beginning

I was born June 12 1982 in Jersey City, New Jersey. My name is Julius Jones. I came from a strong, beautiful woman; my mama Annette Boney Kennedy. If I had to think of one word to describe her it would be invaluable. My mama is truly priceless. I was her first born and they say it was nice weather. You know being born in the very early 80s times were very different especially from now to back then. At this time my father was around. His name is Samuel Jones. My mama was born in Wallace, NC and my father was born in South Carolina.

As a child I was very hyperactive; always into things and always being yelled at because I was always doing something I had no business doing. I could never seem to sit still. I always had to be into certain things which was never good. When I was still in a household with both parents things started changing. Every time you turned around my father was being seen less and less. To his defense though he was always working. He was a Chef. Doing dinner parties was his specialty and he was the best at what he did. Still, behind closed doors things were rough. I have multiple siblings but my mama only had two sons. She wasn't working then still she always made sure home was right. Even with her holding the household down and being head turning gorgeous, that still wasn't enough for my father.

I say that because I have siblings that are the same age as me. Papa was a rolling stone for real. Me and my siblings didn't meet each other till years later because our father was bouncing from house to house dealing with our mothers. Which led to us not meeting some of our older siblings. To this day we still haven't. As my mama started to do more for herself like having her own income & working, my father's attitude towards her started to change.

Because my mother wanted to have her own instead of being dependent on him for everything a lot of arguments started happening. The arguments started left then right, then eventually non-stop especially late at night. I remember one time waking up early in the morning. My father had my mama pinned down on the floor yelling at her. She was shaking her head back and forth because he was spitting on her. He spit on her like she was trash, like she was garbage, like she was nothing. I will never forget that because I had so much rage inside me from seeing that shit.

My mom had this nice wooden brown dresser. It was one of those old-fashioned dressers with thick wood. There was a way you could open it and I broke it in half so I could use it as a weapon to knock the shit out my father. I had it all planned out, I was going to knock the back of his head with it to get him the fuck off my mama & for spitting on her like she was a piece of shit.

For his sake he stopped by the time I actually had the strength enough to break it in half. I was around about 8 or 9 years old.

Around that age, I wanted to be a chef or cook like my father. He was making so much money and it was great career. From that day forward there was no more being under the same roof. No more having two parents. You know as a kid you always try to figure out certain things. You're too young to understand why parents act and move the way they do. Most times you won't figure it out until you get older but by then you are already affected. I didn't receive the proper love because they didn't have that proper love so they couldn't show it.

My mama said back then, she never really said she loved me because when she was growing up her & her siblings didn't hear them words from their own parents. She told plenty of stories about her father always beating on my grandmother Big Mama. Her father was a drunk and wife beater she was born in Wallace, NC. The twisted part is he left all his kids a piece of land but they have yet to claim it. The reason why I am talking and speaking about this subject is so you can see the effects it had on me and others.

I'm getting ahead of myself though, let me get back to my mama. They are from North Carolina, lived out Wallace for a couple of years but Big Mama moved to Jersey City, NJ to get away from their father. My mama started making her own income yet still were struggling. I was twisted because I was moving around a lot with my father. From house to house, City to City and State to State. By the time I moved back with my mama, I never felt like I belong. I felt like I did something wrong because what man would leave his son's and daughter's without finding out they well being the shit turned me so angry and beyond cold.

From that day forward when he dropped me off back to my mama place. I hated seeing kids with their fathers. Like why did everybody else have a father but me and my siblings don't have one. Most of my relatives they had a father around but we didn't. I couldn't stand that shit between that and my mama breaking down over the phone to my big mama. Explaining how she want's to do better, and make more money to make ends meet. To get better things for me and my brother.

Rent is always backed up, sometimes the lights will be cut off and we use candles to see at night. We didn't even have a table or TV stand for the TV we use crates, and iron hanger's that will be used for antenna's. These kids today is so rotten, they spoil and make me sick to my stomach. They don't appreciate shit yet at the same token that comes from these weak ass parents being they friends instead of being a mother and father.

After hearing my mama breakdown twice back to back late at night to my big mama. That's when I decided at the age of ten going on eleven things was going to change. I remember walking to school with my mama. I was 9 years old walking to no.15 school coming from Stegman and Ocean. Seeing a dope fiend that was so high, I told my mama I would never sell drugs. Because I didn't want to be a part of having my own kind, own people that look like me looking like that strung out on drugs.

Being so young at that time and age, I felt I had no other options wish I didn't because I was too young to have a job. Far as my family my mama side, I was always a black sheep. I was always being talked down to left and right. Every time you turn around somebody always had something to say. Yet let one of their kids get into a situation I'll be the first one to be called. Being so young the consequences I never gave a fuck about, it was all about stopping my mama from crying at night. It always did something to my soul, every time repeat that shit. Always thought about in my mind how she sounded on the phone crying to my big mama. You knew my mama was a strong gem, she never broke down once in front of me or my brother.

During them times women back then man mothers were a force beyond strength. I'm proud to say my mama is strong beyond steal. In the very early 90s being so young, every kid wasn't allowed to be on a block as it is today. Street Life wasn't for everybody and that's a major problem that we face today in the world. Let alone street life is not for nobody to be exact. Yet again we talking about ignorance and stupidity and from a street perspective and mindset. You were tested to be on any block any block to be outside especially with certain caliber of older men.

To see if you running your mouth or not being the lookout even going to the store or paying attention, to observe your surroundings, to see how you move on your own. There's none of that once this 2000s new millennium shit start happened. Anybody allowed to be on the block outside even in the gang but yet we going to get to that in a few.

Again in the early 90s it was different different. This cloth you had to be born with this shit. The greatest time. If you were a snitch your ass got whacked, if you were a snitch you didn't come around the block. You knew not to come around because of the repercussions.

Nowadays snitches get all the love, the respect and more shit. They are allowed back on the blocks and making more money and better positions in the mother fucker that stood ten toes down.

I was raised on Stegman and ocean, Stegman life!

Was raised by one of the best to ever do it X-Man, grew up around Wu. Even though Wu was older than me by very few years I looked up to Wu. The way he carried himself, every time a situation was time to put it down he didn't need no help the same for X-Man. It was always me X-Man, Wu, Freaky Ty she's a woman. This when Stegman was Stegman the real Stegman n Ocean. When you had to earn your right to be on Stegman and Ocean. When X-Man got killed Stegman and Ocean crippled. That's when Wu started knocking shit down then, that's when I started raising up.

You can definitely tell older dudes was happy that X-Man was gone because they feared him. Things don't never always have to be said it's the way you move, your actions that speak louder than words. X-Man damn near ran everybody off Stegman n Ocean.

Dead Homies! X-Man was a hot head but a genuine person would give you the shirt off his back. X-Man death did something to me and Wu personally. Believe me before he got killed he tore somebody ass up though. X-Man was my Og, I learned about giving back to the community. Watching X-Man always throwing block parties and cookouts. You see certain older caliber men was always giving back to their own blocks. You have brothers like Bernie D, Ace, boxing Shy they all was from Stegman and Wegman n Jackson. Run from Lexington used to always throw water parks Six Flags Great Adventure bus trips.

God bless the dead Champ from Carrie Woods who used to throw the big ass cookouts. I used to go down Carrie woods every time with X-Man. When X- Man got killed Champ lost his mind because they were brothers. Yet back to Wu though every time you turn around somebody disrespected or looking at somebody from Ocean. Your ass got tore up! Then one day, I guess he was so tired he turn himself in and that's when I unleashed.

Set The Record Straight

You know before this Blood and Crip thing started in Jersey. Killing been going on in Jersey, yeah I must admit this Blood and Crip thing took it to a whole another level of killers. At the time back then in Jersey City, Sex Money Murder were deep and the deepest. Yet they weren't gang bangin when, I mean gang bangin. I mean color bangin going at they rivals. Also had Nine Trey Gangster Bloods yet we stopped them from saying that, they say Tech gang.

Reason why because Trays are Crips. Same for GKB which stands for Gangster Killer Bloods we had them saying G-SHINE. How you Blood got a K in front of B that don't make no sense. You know in the beginning when this Duma Life hit the state of New Jersey, East Orange to be specific. That were Queen Street Bloods to be exact. This was in 1993 yet Fruit Town Brims 36th Street were in the state of New Jersey in 1992 but the seed wasn't implanted yet.

The fool caught a hot one, so he skipped town and went back to West Side South Central L.A. to get his name you can catch it on volume one Invincible Tears Big L Brim speak about his name I don't make snitches irrelevant. Everyone have to understand when we talking about the East Coast, when we talking about this Damu Life this Blood Gang it started in the state of New Jersey. Up North New Jersey Essex County that's where everything landed at and spread out. Queen Street Bloods it transition to Ill Town Double ii Bloods 235.

The Og from Inglewood Queen Street Big Trouble in them was fucking with Treach from Naughty by Nature. This is how they started coming to up north New Jersey dealing with Jersey. You got these silly ass rappers talking about some rap shit. How they went out to Bompton with that "Certified Gangster" video man it's been Jersey since the beginning of time we don't give a damn about that rap shit. We talking about a time when it was real duma love when we were really cK when it comes to this Jersey shit. Then you had the Bix Bix Deuce Mob Piru the Tree Top Piru 400 block.

Yeah the Bloodstone Villains 52nd Street, 5 Line Bounty Hunters Bloods. Fruit Town Brims 36th Street was around yet at the time, when that snitch got extradited back to the state of New Jersey that's some Kutt prison mess. Me personally, I don't count that jail shit and this is all in 1993 when Fruit Town Brims 36th Street was in Jersey state prisons.

The Ill Town Double ii Bloods 235, Massacre in them had something priceless. It was priceless because they built they set from the ground up everybody were from the same block, pretty much grew up together. You see these different Blood sets wasn't made up, it was brought to the state of New Jersey up north. While in New York they read Monster Kody book's and started making up sets. Mind you that book is about a person that's from Eight Tray Gangster Crips.

You see the similarities in Eight Trey Gangsters, Nine Trey Gangsters. I get it they were being oppressed by some Spanish and Latin Kings but what do that have to do with taking on a name Blood that has nothing to do with anything. For three decades been nothing but lies and documentaries and all this extra mess and I'm beyond sick of it.

This isn't just a story this a reality what the fuck goes on in Jersey. During these times everything was up North New Jersey nowhere else. There were only South Central L.A and Compton Inglewood in Watts California gangs in the state of New Jersey at that time. I believe between the end of "95 too 97" that's when fools started riding that five point star from New York. Couple of people were getting locked up in New York in they jails going to cop some work to bring it back to Jersey. In a mix of that, got put on to they sets in New York jails.

You see when it comes to this Duma shit, I respect it wholeheartedly. First generations of being a Blood was like Massacre, Machete, Monster Ru Ali Doorstop, Mobster Ru, Threat, Cock and Squeeze his brother Qua Ru, Twist Ru, Lil Trouble, Sue and the list goes on. Shit when I got put on man it was about that man standing right next to you it was about camaraderie. A sense of belonging brothers feeling the same way as you but yet that is a myth.

Far as on the East Coast anyway but I get to that. You will see for yourself that shit is a myth. You should always find out and know when you get put onto something and become a part of it. You should always want to know the truth, the history because otherwise you just a follower and a wannabe. In life we all follow somebody the difference is you follow somebody to become greater to learn to get an understanding not to do the same things, that was done before you.

To do better, now if you following this to be following. You don't know what you doing that's what makes you a follower. Because you have no understanding to be understood what you are representing. Truthfully the average person on the East Coast don't no a damn thing about what being a Damu is let alone the history of they own sets. For starters the word Blood down, have no meaning no Ackerman. There's no break down, there is no such thing as Brotherly Love Overrides Oppression. That's something that is made up.

The word Blood is how we can identify one another when we are in prison. Crips dominated us as individual sets before creating the blood Banner. What, I mean is that we had to come up with a name that unified us as individual sets. So, we can survive in California State Prisons let alone the bounty. For every 10 Crips there were only one Blood.

Again though in Jersey this when it was a time to be proud to be a Damu West Coast set. We didn't have numbers yet we had strength the more numbers the more weaker the less numbers the more strength. Let me just double back real quick back on New York tap in back to that ass. The world and everybody needs to know this, if they started what they call Bloods in New York on Rikers Island. That was done because they were being oppressed by Latin Kings that's originally from Chicago.

So, why would they all fall underneath a nation as representing a five point star if it was really about sticking together and being black. There's no excuse that means you show a sign of weakness. Bloods and Crips been going on over five Decades. Us Bloods always been outnumbered we never fell under being strictly Crips. Not as a whole, it feeds the purpose and it is disrespectful to those that paved the way and died for you.

The first generation much love and respect they paved the way for me to represent this Blood Gang. Shit my generation, second generation shittttt. We were volunteering dead homies. Make no mistake this isn't to be glorified but these kids need to know what they getting themselves into. These young teenagers need to know what they signing up for when it come to this Damu Life! You had Brims in Jersey City yet during that time, they wasn't about nothing.

They was on Bostwick n Jackson. All they did was get drunk and high smoke dust and dip all day. It change quick once Bull stepped on the scene. He was militant dedicated and put in a mad work but yet at the same token he can think. Even though their were Fruit Town Brims 36th Street on Bostwick n Jackson and reality Bull set the tone and stamp it on Stegman n Ocean. No other blood sets were cK until Fruit Town Brims 36th Street stepped on the scene.

Everyone was dressing all pretty and cute. Wearing brand-new flags left and right. You may have had very few, selected few from different sets that did they thang. I'm talking about as a whole as a unit Fruit Town Brim to be exact. Bull was laying that shit down right. Nobody can say different. No other sets in Jersey City at this time was riding on other sets let alone Crips. Fools were on goofy time in riding on, popping on anybody because they had on the color blue.

I remember 2 people from Sex Money Murder tried that mess with one of my nephews. On West Side Brims I walked right up on Wegman n Ocean put a big trey pound right to buster stomach. Blood snitched on his homie right in front of his other homie Body from his set. On West Side Brims if it wasn't for Body intervene and I really knew Blood. And I knew Blood personally that intervene. I locked eyes with Blood the whole time, I was there my big trey pound seven was right on his stomach, I would have left his ass right where he stood at. Blood kept talking about he apologize, I just walked off and ran into the other buster that he snitched on about.

He actually knew, I was coming to look for his ass and he apologized immediately on the set. If anyone of them were really with this shit, you could identify a real Crip. How they stance, they tattoos they aura. In most importantly a real Crip never will denied they shit. You'll be surprised how many people denied they shit Bloods and Crips.

Not proud what they representing but got the nerve to be on social media still claiming. Honestly before Blood hit Jersey City hard in particular a lot of these fools wasn't off the porch. Before that they were scared to be outside. In the same breath this shit still tested a lot of fools heart. In see where they rely at when it came to this Blood Gang you'll see.

Bull was putting in so much work, the gang task force was riding around with a picture of him every night. One night gang task stop my little relative Reek and told him if he ever see Bull for him to contact them. So they can get him off the streets. At the same token, I was telling Bull to be easy cause at this time. I was in the program / halfway house almost about to be out. It was a person in particular I was concerned about that I knew he wasn't built for this shit.

When, I was informed what took place with BG and Bull. When, I found out the person that was picked up for questioning I knew instantly I told Bull I'm a down that buster. Blood was on some Kickback shit like Blood isn't going to snitch. At the same time he told homicide detectives that everybody were Bloods in that area the night shit went down. Now you have homicide detectives looking for Bull and shit he didn't snitch but yet he still shouldn't have said that shit in the first place. Before Bull get locked up, I remember he was knocking out some fools that was on Rough Riders Label.

They was saying they were Crips. Once Bull get locked up slowly that's when, I was making my way home. Before BG got locked up when it was on site between Fruit Town Brims and Tech gang. Dip Set decide performing live one night in Jersey B G went right on the stage and knocked out Juelz Santana. In Jersey we don't give a fuck about that shit , we riding an dying behind this shit.

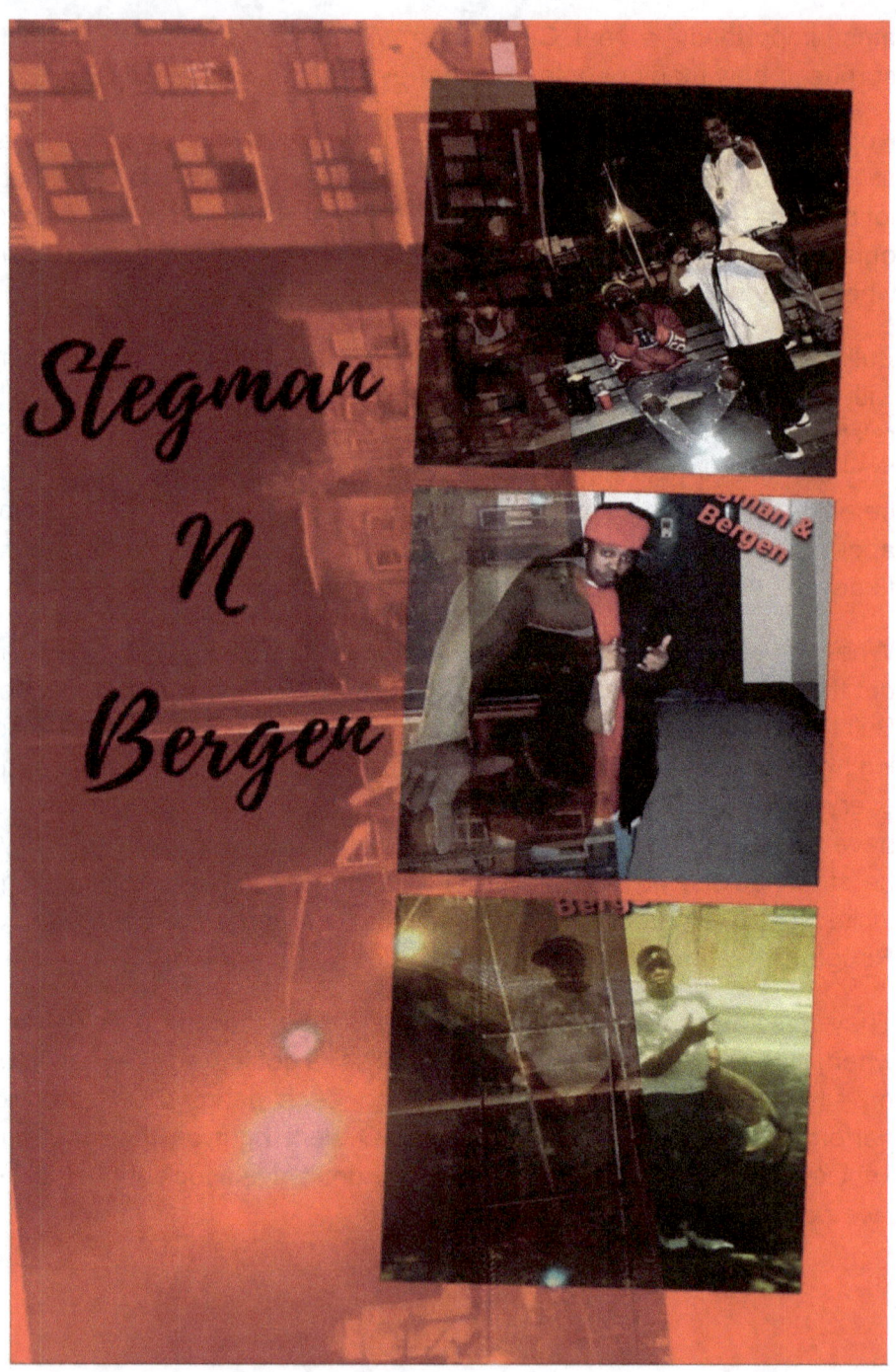

The Tone Was Definitely Set

I'm finally home now homies need bail money, lawyer money and some more shit. Everyone informing me what happened but nobody have no type of ends. In at the same time, I have a daughter on the way, also my oldest daughter Princess and another little girl, I was taking care of at the time. Yeah, I had to get right to it though. You had homies checking for lawyers, didn't have no ends though. Bull informing me who was going to give up money. These fools was broke, they were worried about they damn self. I gave fools a solid month after that, I was taking care of everything.

This when, I first met Kaoss, he pulled up with Mr. 187 and two other fools. They pulled up at a place that, I was at. Soon as I stepped out the house and he said my name to the homie from Newark and Irvington New Jersey. They started laughing. They was laughing because I was told how Bull and Mr. 187 in the rest used to talk about me all the time. They said the way homies was talking about me like I was tall like Killa E., Mr. 187 all he said was like alright you'll see.

That same night we went out to cK. By time the homie found a parking space, I was out the car already knock a rip down was headed back to the car. By time the homies even got out the car. After that shit we went to go get some 40oz and went to Crenshaw. We call Crenshaw the Crown's Chicken right next to Lincoln High School. Back then if you was really a Blood pressing the line, you met at Crenshaw. Another place we called Crenshaw was out in Irvington New Jersey off of Lyons Avenue White Castle's straight death trap. Different type of Crip sets run that spot.

That was a difference between the two and Jersey City it was Damu. Mr. 187 he was a worker, he was never no hustler. Shit he was putting in more work then the fools was actually out there on the block. I say that to say this that month was up and fools still didn't have shit towards no homies lawyers. I was still going back and forth out of town making money.

It was Fruit Town Brims on Stegman n Bergen as well as Arlington Park. There were only a few of us. We were the loudest though when you talk about back to back knocking shit down man it was Fruit Town Brims 36th Street. BRIM GANG or DON'T BANG at this time I met a fool from Hoboken but I made his ass come on the hill, he acted like he was scared. Bull said he was selling a lot of dust yet I wasn't impressed.

The whole point of Blood coming from Hoboken to the hill was to help put money together for the homies. Me personally, I didn't need nobody I'm just being honest. Of course, I wasn't nowhere rich but shit I had it. The whole time this fool were on some shit of having homies just to sell his shit and make more money. Manika Mane was right there when I told Blood get the fuck from the hill before I, do something to you. From then on we moving around, then homies started going out with me and my brother Tai' Quwan. Shit we go cK then go out to Cheetahs or Club NV. Every time we went out to New York, I was always looking for a fool that was riding the 5 pushing a Brim set. No L.A gangs ride the five or the six, it's just the right and the left. Five point star represent People Nation six point star represent Folk Nation. That migrated from Chicago gangs has nothing to do with L.A gangs. The six flag on the right and the 5 flag on the left. No Debate....

Back to this West Side Fruit Town Brims 36th Street gang. When, I slow down from going back and forth, going out of town into making money. Me and Mr. 187 all we was doing was going on missions hell of missions. These mother fools really don't have a clue. Again at the time it was only about like 11 or 12 of us the most. Everyone needs to no everybody isn't a killer or a rider. 75% of every set most are ornaments looking pretty for the Christmas tree.

I got put on to get active fuck that pretty shit. Dressing up just to look a part with the dickey's suit in the chucks on that's just a costume. If you aren't really putting in work and getting that shit dirty. What, I mean by dirty is blood on your shit. Day and night! It was on I had that money up ASAP for a lawyer. Only 2 homies had put up $300 a piece, I put up the rest which was $6,300 the lawyer all together he wanted $10,000.

Another homie said he was going to put up $300 when his income tax came. Long story short that fool spent that shit on jewelry and clothes.

Every time you turnaround he had something new on talking about his woman bought that shit. Everyone scream out that loyalty and love shit, when really they be about themselves. I had got that shit out the way from the door I put over $300 in Blood account. His codefendant I put over $100. Nobody wasn't putting up shit. Fools saying otherwise they are lying dead homies. I was sending another homie money every week but the woman he called his woman she was keeping the shit getting her hair done. I remember one night we went out to the club with my sister Erica and her girlfriends as a matter of fact the home girl Marcy. All, I know is that I came out the bathroom from inside the club and went outside.

Seeing Mr. 187 in another homie and my sister Erica and Marcy fighting some clowns. I push Mr. 187 out the way once I knocked the mark out. I started slowly stomping on his temple every time his head bounce off the ground. I got bored with that quickly by the time I looked up my sister Erica knew to throw me the keys so I can go right to the car. I was going get my gun so I can lay both of them fools down. Then a woman kept saying you all better leave the police coming the police are coming. Mr. 187 he came off with a chain I was mad as shit, I didn't get to lay them clowns down for smacking my sister on the ass.

The next day, I made sure I gave it to somebody else though on Brim Gang.

I was different different with this shit. I remember we had a on site with Tech gang because they killed the first Brim homie Fruit Town Brick City Brim 232 Doo Doo. The very first Brim homie that were actually killed from Newark. I have Blood tatted on me, after he was killed nine of them got killed. Back to back to back to back to back to back to back we went back-to-back so much they waved a white flag ASAP Dead Homies! Fruit Town Brims 36th Street and Fruit Town Brick City Brim 232 step on the scene we change the whole gang world.

I say that to say us Westside brims we are responsible pursuing the five point stars issue. New York Brim sets was trying to migrate in Jersey

City and Trenton New Jersey. In we was popping they asses left and right no talking or nothing just dropping them. There's no false flagging coming with this Damu Life. How New York talking they Brim in they set not from L.A or Branch off. Talking about they 59 brims from New York and started in 95 that's false. 59 BRIMS started on 59th Street before it was 59 Hoover Crips. In that's on the West Side of South Central L.A back then most of west of South Central L.A were different Brim sets. 59 brims was moved to San Diego after Lil cK Kountry

B.I.P was killed by Westside Crips.

Again you can check out who Lil cK Kountry is, his picture is in "Invincible Tears Vol 1". When, I was out there on Stegman n Bergen we didn't sell no drugs in front of the elderly and kids. We held the door for them if they had groceries most importantly we brought the groceries inside they home. During these times fools were scared to be Brim you had to put in work you had to rip ride. No disrespect to any rip riders but this what was going on during my time of gang bangin.

I was graze by a bullet by a rip on the right side of my temple. Different Crip sets in particular 103rd Grape Street Gangster Crips and Rollin 60s Crips they used to catch homies bailing out the bounty gunning homies down and leaving they bodies on the highway. Another place they used to catch homies slipping was the movie theaters. Cee Blaze from 103rd Grape Street Gangster Crips he did some gangster shit. Blood was a target in hot topic homies was definitely trying to get his head.

So, one afternoon in broad daylight Cee Blaze pulls up to a Blood set hops out with the gun in hand tell them to fallback, they were planning on rushing him. Cee Blaze walk to the trunk of his car and pops the trunk open in the back it's they homie butt ass naked tied up with a sock in his mouth. Blood put that gun right to the homie head and told his homies if you don't stay off my ass I'm going to blow his shit off right now.

Cee Blaze got back in the car in drove off and kicked the homie out his trunk. Booda Hat rolled past some Sex Money Murder on Ocean and Wegman. They was flagging when them Sex Money Murder saw Booda Hat they automatically tuck they flags in. Booda Hat get out the car in tell the Sex Money Murder homies to take they flags back out they pockets and better never tuck they flags back in when they see him represent that shit be proud.

He get back in his car and drove off, he was from 5 Deuce Hoover Crips got put on right on his turf. Trust a lot of Crips were doing a lot of bK (Blood Killing) no that I'm just a Brim telling his story. May sound awkward but I was gang bangin and making money. Eventually one will pull me more then the other. I remember we went out to club Exit I believe on 57th Street in New York. That night was definitely bracken before we go there the homies have a little whoop about me. Not to be on no set tripping shit that's all, I liked to do. Set tripping I just love that shit. Brim Gang or Don't Gang....

Before we go in there, I agree just to stop hearing the complaining about how I set trip everywhere we go. On dead homies soon we get in there I just see hella Crips. It was actually Neighborhood Rollin 60s Crips from the Neighborhood o card. One of our main rivals. Once I seen that shit, I started throwing up cK in they faces nigha.. that shit is a adrenaline rush on the set. I started B Walking in everything and Manika Maine follow suit. He wasn't B walking he doesn't know how but he was throwing it up cK chunky I'm not going lie though that shit lasted about a good 5 or 7 minutes. Out of nowhere it was so many goddamn Rollin 60s Crips that it was ridiculous. They all were from Long Island we got the fuck up out of there laughs....

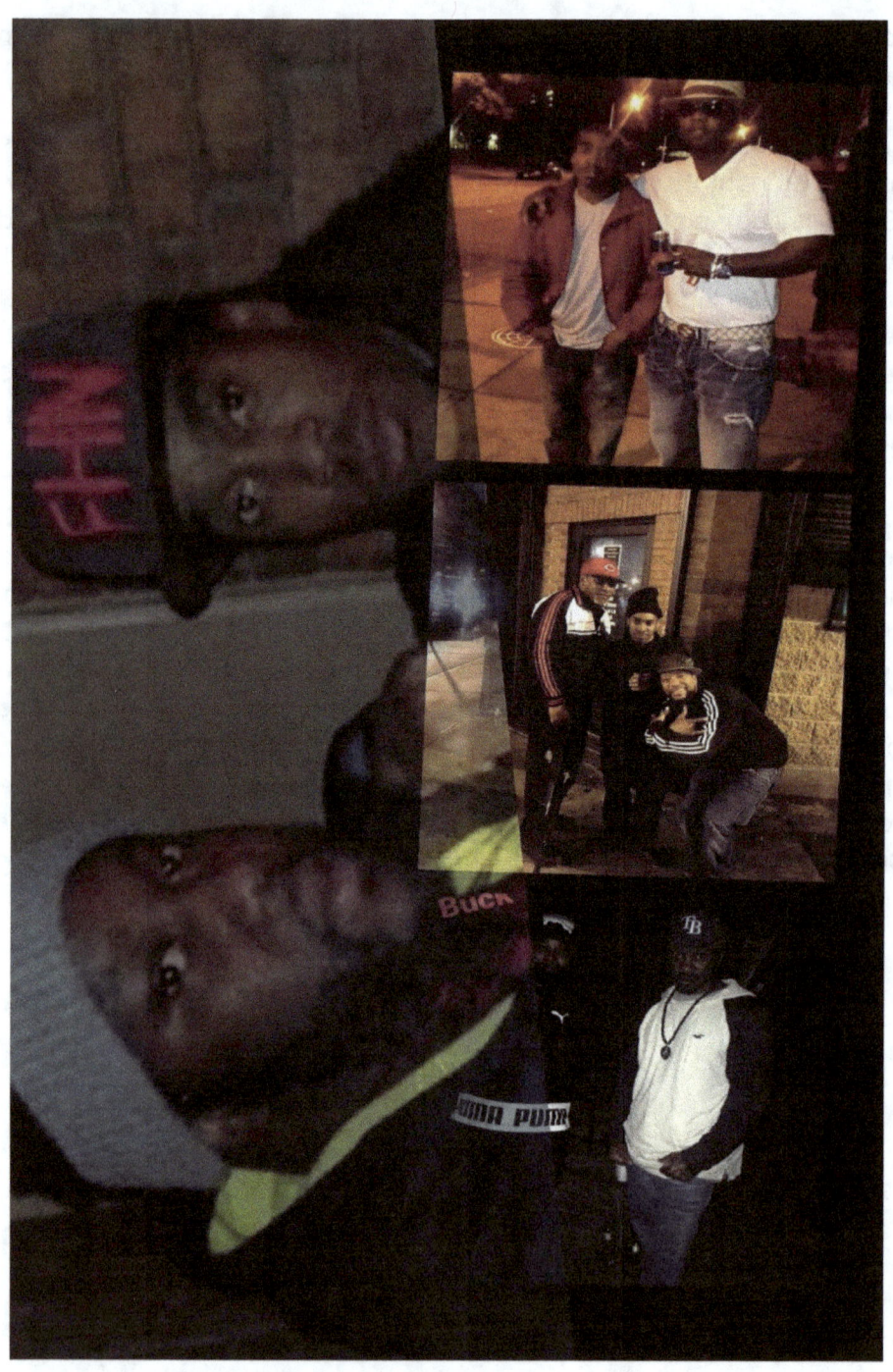

Back Down Memory Lane

Every time, I turn around I was always waking up in cold sweats. Face and eyes always on fire. Most of the times, I kept my hand in my pocket and finger on the trigger just in case anybody ever thought coming through that door. Sometimes my mama would catch the gun pointing at my head as I was sleeping. That would only happen when, I slept with my gun under my pillow.

Any woman, I dealt with I would always have a gun under my pillow. I always kept a revolver because it was the best murder weapon. The shells never dropped to hit the ground everyone with them dumbass extended clips in want to keep shooting just looking for attention. This shit was do or die get in and get out. You see back then people knew the name just couldn't match the face I was a ghost. One of the easiest ways to get wack was being too loud looking for attention. Be the same ones that be snitches anyway.

Every morning, I woke up I recite my history might have a triple black Beretta with the full black dickie suit on. Another day may have Chrome nickel plated nine with sky blue jeans on, everywhere I went my finger was never away from that trigger. I never gave myself a name everybody else always called me Gunna, Mr. Gun Play, Walk Ups even O Dogg for some situations that happened in broad day at the end of the day it still all add up to the same person Lil Wild Ju from Stegman n Ocean....

A lot of fools be having names just to have name or to sound tuff and don't have no murders or Crip killings! Every time, I looked at my mama eyes they were always sad and worried. Between time through trials and tribulations and era.

I stay dedicated to being a loving father first. Every night, I tuck my oldest daughter Princess in bed Bathe her and read her bedtime stories. If, I wasn't picking her up from school I was waiting for her to get home from school. I would always take her to the park in the movies. Every time it would be snowing I would have snowball fights with her and little friends and my little niece that sometimes call me dad. That was my shorty, shorty 140 E'Shyna. It was nothing like being a father it made me feel human. In then came Julissa my daughter I call her Angel. I named her after me. She was so attached to me that the only way she would go to sleep if she hear my voice.

Princess was proud to be a big sister still in all I had this other little girl I was taking care of for two years and come to find out she wasn't even my daughter. The cold part she learned her first words calling me Daddy and took her first steps walking to me at Buck and Ebony house.

Speaking of Buck, Buck was one of the very first people that told me, I need to stop putting my life on the line for these fools saying they wasn't built. Same goes for my brother Naim and my brother Tai Quwan it was a lot of older heads was upset I even got put on in the first place. By the time homies came outside I was already a elite being an non-affiliated.

Even though I was still young I was just outside way before them. I didn't need no bandana to come outside this shit didn't make me no disrespect. It's just what it is! Back to that little girl though that shit fucked me up when I found out she wasn't mine. Only reason that even happen her mama was on some spiteful shit. I didn't want to be with her I'm not dealing with nobody I don't trust. So, she wanted to take me to child support for that reason. I'm given this girl $250 a month and every two weeks buying everything under the sun for that little girl. As well paying my sister Erica to take me to pick her up she lived two hours away.

Having the money to get a car wasn't the issue, the problem was I didn't have no license. Back in those times if you had a violent crime your license was suspended for 7 years in the state of New Jersey. My shit stayed suspended truthfully. Even though I'm in the streets, I still think smart move strategically.

I used to go to Law Library to find out how to get away with different crimes. You know after you bust a gun, the gun powder get on your hand so, I always carry a little bleach bottle. If, I ran out I made myself piss, right on my hand that always did the trick. Back to that little girl, I was extremely hurt. Two years of my life down the drain wasn't even about the money, that was nothing it was more about my oldest daughter Princess and Mama.

This is actually my first time speaking about this whole situation publicly. Till this day I still really didn't take the time to really digest that shit. Any way, back at my mama house I'm finally getting dressed. First person, I run into Ski Bop he always dropping some jewels but he did question me having these homies around me. We haven't seen each other in a while yet that day we had a nice little talk. Just saying don't get caught up and trap off spend the rest of your life in prison.

Then right after that, I ran into Calone. In Calone got straight to the point, I know you not listening to them niggas and following orders. I lock eyes with Calone smirk like hell no, the average person have the wrong misconception of what being a Blood is.

Nobody tell you what to do and if so you're buster. There's no such thing as status there's no such thing as speaking in codes. Definitely not wearing them religion bees don't have anything to do with being a Blood. All that 5 poppin 6 dropping that is Chicago. If you don't know your history use a wannabe just because you know your history don't make you a real one or real blood. If you claiming a West Coast set doesn't make you official.

Back to Calone, I listen at the end of the day that's who helped raise me, when it comes to this street life same goes for Ski Bop. My brother Naim that was another story, he was definitely on my ass when it came to me being a Blood. I understand too be fully understood. I was his little brother and most importantly it was the same situation as everybody else you don't need to be in no gang. We wasn't talking for a while for that reason. I used to always go out of town when he was in Delaware. He knew the way I was moving it was the very reason him being on my ass about being a Blood. I had got put on back then but it wasn't the correct way.

When Killa E hard headed ass follow P Nutt. I don't know why he even did that shit in the first place. He was always about himself. I was even upset when he had did that shit. Truth be told our family alone a gang no extras. I'm talking about the caliber of men in our family. I was always around Grunt and Snoop, people always thought Grunt was my older brother.

Even before Black went down we were always around each other. We are all related I remember one night Snoop told me some shit. Matter fact it wasn't even at night, it was during the afternoon. It was a situation going on with him and some fool off Ocean.

The situation he had with the person, I knew he was bool he telling me I don't got nothing to do with it. Not in anyway that he was going to do something to me. More like I just came on the scene, I don't know what is going on. Snoop wanted to shoot his ass up but I told him I got a better idea. I'm like Blood don't even no we actually related.

That same night me and Mr. 187 we on some bikes he got a foe pound I had a 22 rifle with a scope. Into we clear that whole shit. Right after that we took our asses through Stegman Wegman n Ocean. Reason being the night before Bo Rock told me some other shit fools was playing down there. Shit, I took the opportunity to see how much they really wanted to play then. When fools seen that long shit on my lap when I was on that little ass bike. All you heard was crickets. Before that we was coming from down Neptune and Ocean way paying a little visit somebody disrespected my sister Erica. By time we got down their Ron G got that fool up out of their. When me and Mr. 187 rides up on the bikes Ron G started immediately complaining.

Like I called you and told you don't come down here, I'm going to take care of it I started laughing I'm like by time you called me I was already damn near here. When my sister calls, I'm not wasting no time with nobody. Your sister no different from your mama as well your daughters and nieces. Blood got up out of there like Flash Gordon though laughs.

Another time with Ron G that fool had somebody selling our dope. Blood gets locked up then Ron G bails him out, Ron G balls my phone and tells me that, the fool on some bullshit. He just going to bick it he's not going to try to come up with the money. The money that was lost for the product and getting his ass out of jail. I told Blood Ron G bring that fool on Stegman n Bergen.

I believe it was around 8 or 9 at night right where everybody can see what I was about to do. Soon when, I walked up he's smiling and having his hand out. I immediately pulled out the snub-nosed thirty-eight put it towards his temple. Looking right in his eyes in told Blood like fool you tripping you going to get our money back. Guess what I laughs he got that mother fucking money back ignorance and stupidity I could have went about it in a respectful way.

Young hotheaded full of cum. It was this one time though I went to Multiplex Cinemax in Newark that movie theater was controlled by 103_{rd} Grape Street Gangster Crips. I'm talking about from little toddlers to grand mamas would have purple flags on and little kids C walking in the theater. I call myself going out with a young lady at the time and forgetting I have on red laces shoe strings. Immediately the 103_{rd} Grape Street Gangster Crips spotted my laces in started calling me a "Slob" I was so tight.

The word "Slob" is a disrespectful word towards the bloods. The young lady started asking me why they keep saying "Slob" my rely was my shoelaces. She held to my arm tighter and my hand on the trigger I wanted to shoot Blood in his mouth so bad. We go to see our movie, yet theirs a fool inside the movie theater throwing up Blood and his set. I'm like he got to be tripping or high he definitely don't know where he at or just suicide. The Grape Streets waited to Blood got comfortable and shot him in back of his head. It use to be a well known projects name "Hyatt Courts" right by the movie theater. Everyone in the projects was 103_{rd} Grape Street Gangster Crips between these times.

Those was the times and days the last of the authentic era followers back then was our rivals. Today they rather have followers on social media. I'm just finding out what opp is and I'm trying to figure out what that got to do with being a Blood or a Crip. This thing of ours, our culture of being a Damu it's a disgrace. I'll leave that alone for later though let me get back to my story.

Things Come Too A End

By this time Stegman n Bergen was the home front for Fruit Town Brims 36th Street. Audubon Park is where we had our w36p or sometimes Bayside Park. Audubon Park was home though. Bickin it putting in work having basketball games 5 on 5 with different sets. Like with Sex Money Murder or 464 Insane Mob Piru just to name a few....

I remember one night with me Mr. 187 another homie we happen to look down the block a fool was Crip walking in the middle of the street at night. Like this fool don't no where he at Mr. 187 got right up on him. Put the gun to him asked him was he a real Crip he said no he was just watching a video came outside and started Crip walking.

I was pissed the hell off I shook my head and walked off. Like these kids and young teens don't have a clue what they getting themselves into. Truth of the matter even adults the next day though around 1 p.m. me and Mr. 187 we outside its hot as hell.

Some fool bold enough to wear purple laces purple flag and all of that. We couldn't believe our eyes like we had to double look at each other than look at him. Like he must want to die, Mr. 187 got right up on him smack him with his burner. I got right up on him, grab my gun and stuff it right in his mouth. Mr. 187 burnt his flag and we stripped his ass butt naked. To celebrate we went to go get some Ol English.

By this time 464 Insane Mob Piru got shot, even though he wasn't a Fruit Town Brims 36th Street. He was still Blood though even more so Westside. Back then up north in Jersey that's how we roll any West Coast set. If one pop we all pop, it isn't like that at all Bloods killing Bloods a disgrace how can you say you love that red flag when you killing another homie. Everyone should just be Crips. Crips been doing that shit since 1979.

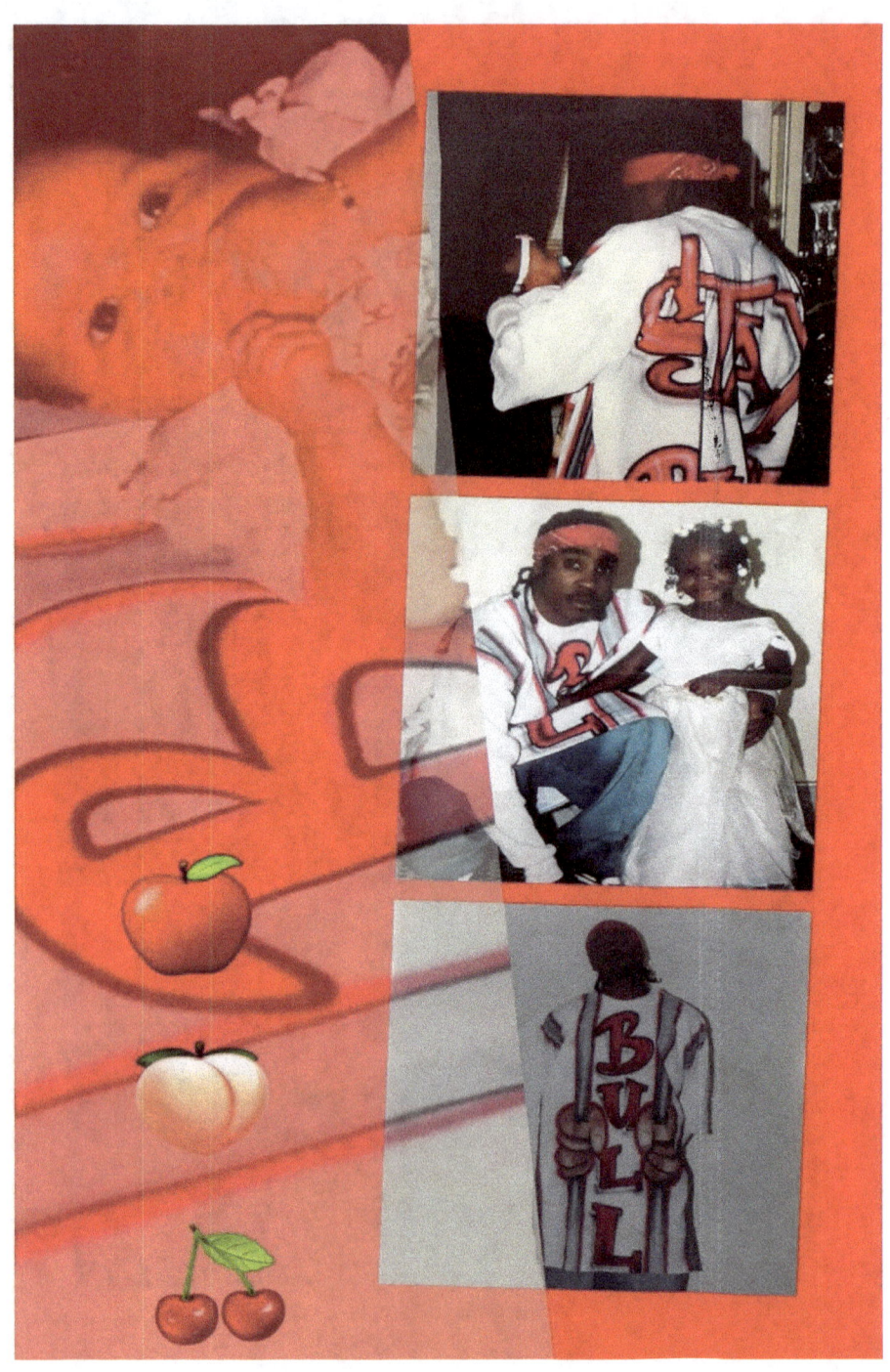

Back to this fool getting shot though. I ask the homies like what type of time Blood on. We not just risking our life and freedom when he isn't even on the same time. If Blood move then I'm in other than that this West Side Fruit

Town Brims 36th briminal that's Piru business. After a few days Blood in the process of healing up between that time though, I told Blood like. I got a funny feeling about Blood. He better not hesitate dead homies.

By this time No Exit tell me about Spazz, how he was always tripping a little hot head. Wu nephew. I didn't put Blood on but Blood made decision becoming Brim he heard I was Brimin. In Jersey City no one man were bigger than the other no one person made the decision to put anyone on. The second anyone decided to put anyone on by themselves. That meant they thought they were bigger than the program. How one man of many can make a decision for the set. (If we are a family, a family make a decisions together).

But that's the problem now, I would get back to that later. I told No Exit after we handle this situation we going bick it with Blood. Spazz just needed the proper guidance but other than that he was really tearing shit up. A lot of fools that were older than him and before him didn't do shit. If they did they felt obligated to do so. That shit don't count in my book and stripes isn't yours. The 464 Insane Mob Piru homie pulls up, every one acting like they ready to ride. I told everyone if they hesitate I'm knocking they shit off. That's a sign right there that they going to snitch now you see hesitation getting in that damn car....

We riding around getting couple of shots off. Me personally I'm not with that riding around it's walk-ups. I be the last face that you see every time I went I was bare face anyway. Finally I had enough of that I'm like Blood pull the fuck over fool we hopping out. As I'm walking to a food stand a homie grab me like we not doing it like that.

 Finally we found our targets at least, I thought fools were on the same page. Its 5 to 6 of these fools sitting on the porch it's wide open for me to take advantage. As soon I'm lifting my arm up to spray the whole porch, the Piru homie stop me talking about he think the police coming like how do you think theirs police coming when I look nobody driving down the block. We went to another area but I stayed in the car I was mad as shit.

In, I still didn't hear no shots the area they went to. It was enough of this shit, I said they all be at this one house. You won't believe this shit 464 Insane Mob Piru homie going say lets wait till they come outside. I'm like what we waiting for we could just go in and lay everybody down. I told Blood drop me off and lose my number anybody dealing with that fool stay the hell away from me dead homies. Got me on a circus chase fake ass mission.

It's bad enough I got queens depending on me. I'm out here running around with a fool on some faking shit. Like right after that we had a huge blow. The next day Dead Wrong and J Vito came up there and bick it with us for a few on Stegman and Bergen. It was a celebration for Dead Wrong birthday as well they were about to get sign J Vito he was that nice to Block Royal Records. At the time that wasn't Akon record label. It was left to him after his manager was killed down ringside.

Back to what, I was saying during that day me and Mr. 187 told them we wanted to go. We will follow them including my brother Tai Quwan they were going out to Harlem New York to celebrate Dead Wrong birthday. Me and Mr. 187 just waiting on the phone call, so we can meet up down in Arlington Park.

We never received that phone call, we wasn't tripping about it we just hope they be safe. Like 4 something in the a.m. I got a phone call Mr. 187 like J Vito got killed. My response was like don't hit me back to anyone find out who did that shit. Our very first loss it felt like it was more than one homie. I wasn't shedding tears, my tears coming from empty clips in the barrel of smoking gun. It took a few days for us to find out who is responsible word was Harlem 30s Crips did that shit our number one rivals.

The day of his funeral everybody doing this fake weeping crying fake tough shit. I spaz out after the funeral like anybody claim they really with this shit pull up on Bergen and let's go. No Exit got a 40 Cal Mr. 187 got the SK and I got the AK-47. Nobody never showed up no call or nothing straight folded Arlington Park was all bluff.

They all went to a fight in Atlantic City, New Jersey No Exit ask me did somebody call I just walked away. From that point on, I was on my own missions. Anyone said something wrong about Brim look at us wrong you were getting gunned down. I was doing favors for favors even dressing up like rips. I was going back to back to back to back....

In after all that shit. It was Tech Gang. I speak about the situation how it all take place in the club and the first book Invincible Tears Volume 1. Blood really had talent in that music shit.I use to go to whoops with all type of Blood on my shirt coming from missions. I must admit that some of the dumbest shit I ever did. I really miss J Vito though Blood. A little after that homies from Paterson name HBo in homies pulls up to Jersey City.

Before they hit Stegman n Bergen, they pulled up to the Bostwick n Jackson. Before all the homies in home girls to fully get out there car the homies on Bostwick ran off. That shit had everybody tight like anybody going to be looked upon like that. By this time its a fool from Hoboken up there too. Talking like he a big homie when he knows nothing about the hood let alone he didn't do shit besides hiding in them damn projects in Hoboken.

I'm not going to front HBo was speaking like we wasn't doing shit like nobody wasn't putting it down. This what he said he was being told. This the very first time we actually really got the chance to really bick it. We've met yet it was very brief, Blood was a front liner. Mr. 187 in the homie they started the conversation, I instantly didn't like how the conversation was going though.

Like Fruit Town Brims 36th street in Jersey City, not putting shit down like we straight ornaments or some shit. After I said this situation that situation that situation and this situation. That's all you heard was Fruit Town Brims. We was going so hard we had other sets throwing up Brim. When we walk up and down the hill fools said the Brims are coming. There were nobody fucking with the Brims fools tripping.

This at the time when Double ii Bloods and West Side Brims were together. We had each other's backs like night and day. There were times you couldn't tell a D i separate from a brim. Back then it was on site whoever was riding the five. Vise versa whoever was pushing a west coast set. One night I was bickin it with my sister Erica, about how I'm tired of this hustling shit.

Through all that I used to always speak about doing events and things like that for the kids at a center. We always ate together did cookouts. Every weekend I use to buy the kids ice creams Crown's Chicken whatever they wanted to eat in that area Audubon Park. We never allow any kid to be harm in that area. I remember one day it was like 2 something in the afternoon. For some damn reason, I'm the only one outside something went down with one of my little relatives and his friends. I just know it was a big ass crowd little older then my little relative and another man that had me by a few years.

So the older guy spoke his piece, then went on and on about how he just got out of prison for attempted murder. The whole time I'm looking right in his eyes. I'm saying in my head I would down this fool right now my finger on the trigger....

It's always the most arrogant fools willing to get killed. After I let him spill his heart I get straight to the point dead homies, I don't care about none of that shit. Theirs nothing happen to my little relative or none of these kids up here on Stegman n Bergen my relative Keisha is outside. The whole time my finger right on this trigger ready to let loose in Broad day. We shook hands peacefully and they went their separate ways. One day I'm walking up to Stegman n Bergen Tai Quwan was really snapping.

I still don't really know what set him off he really was a knockout artist in a real way. I know the first words that came out of his mouth is like all these hating ass niggas they hating on you. The second he feel they trying to do some other shit he going to do something to them. I immediately put my hand in my right pocket that's where, I always kept my snub nose at.

Tai Quwan instantly seen my hand where it was going at and he changed the subject. Tai would knock you out before he use a gun. He will use it though. By this time, I'm out on two separate bills $200,000 and $250,000. I remember before Manika Maine got put on, he told me he was thinking about getting put on to the set. I told him straight up it's not always about who you grew up with, at the same time are your homies going have your back through thick and thin. When Blood do get put on he wanted to use the marker little one eight seven.

I asked him have he ever caught one. Don't be like the rest of these fools. Getting a name because that shit sound tough. Have a name you going live up to other than that you will be a buster. Down the line he understood what I meant. One night I'm sitting at the bench at Audubon Park, same night I believe that Dead Wrong was performing with the murder Mommies being a host at the time they were the biggest thing on Hot 97 105.1.

I was bickin it with Mr. 187 it was another homie to this day, I still don't know who that third person was. I say to Mr. 187 do you feel like cK tonight. He says with a smirk back do you feel like cK I'm like hell yeah I'm like Blood go get the SK I'm grab the AK-47. He had the big foe pound I had the snub nose 38. Tai Quwan said he isn't trusting nobody he wasn't allowing nobody in the car but Mr. 187. He knew what was going to take place that's why he said what he said.

We shoot down Arlington Park I haven't been out the car no more than a minute if that. Next thing you know I heard Gunna watch out you had over 30 something Federal gang task force agents come in my direction from every angle. Mr. 187 ran through the park to get away but I ran the opposite direction to get away. It was just nice parking lot with a high gate and I knew if I could just make it to that parking lot to get over that gate I will be gone.

Me not paying attention and me reaching for my gun to pull it out aim it at the detective by time I realize I'm about to run into a pal of garbage. By the time I try to catch my step and jump over the garbage it was too late I fell. As I'm reaching for my gun it was loose from my hand the detective put his foot on my wrist to stop me from grabbing my gun. Him and his partner pull me up punch me dead in my mouth. As, I looked across the street at Arlington Park.

It was so many people laying on the ground, everyone was going to the same destination. I just had a feeling that was going to be the last time I see Arlington Park for a while. Gang Task Force Federal Unit take me back of homicide behind Dunkin Projects. Immediately I see my picture in a frame on the homicide wall. Once they repeated what I said supposedly at Audubon Park. I knew I was in for a ride. They started answering my phone telling people I wasn't coming home no time soon but little did I know they were right.

HUDSON COUNTY JAIL

The whole time, I'm in the precinct homicide kept talking about two murders that suppose to be on my gun. The wild part the whole time I was there I was trying to figure out. How did they even know, I was coming down there let alone what I had on. They only came for me even though Mr. 187 got away and I was supposed to have two hot ones on that snub-nosed thirty-eight. They already knew what type of gun I like using and carrying.

I get sent to the county I'm trying to figure out who the he'll snitched on me. As soon as I work on trying to rearrange my life this shit happen. In what I meant by rearranging like, I mentioned before I had a nice talk with my sister Erica about quit hustling. By the time, I was sixteen I felt like I was in my late 40s ripping and running I knew I needed to change. It wasn't the hustling honestly it was the gang bangin.

I had recently sign up for this free construction class depending on you, you could graduate 6-9 months I was making it, that was my motivation. I was even looking at nice places out of Pennsylvania two floor condominium. At the same time I couldn't blame nobody but myself the choices in the decisions that I made. I'm in Hudson County Jail I get to D100 right before population some fool I've never seen in my life talking about he Fruit Town Brim and he related to Killer E all I did was shake my head like this fool a groupie my first time meeting a person that got put on in jail let alone on some groupie shit.

Later that day Killa E I met 5 Bix and Babe Head Bussa they both was from Newark New Jersey. Homies were upset very upset that I got re arrested, even homies I just met from Newark was upset. I was the only homie making sure homies had lawyer fees commissary money and sending pics. One homie was like that's all you heard was your name and Mr. 187 name. The very next morning my lawyer shows up at first he was saying some good news. Ask me if, I was trying to get a 4 wit 18 months 4 wit 2 yeas or 3 wit 18 months he left.

I'm all smiling and shit in my head, I'm already planning to get back out there. Mind you the lawyer suppose to came the following week, he came the very next day. I'm like damn that was quick so what you got for me. As soon he opened his mouth the first thing he mentioned was that snub-nosed thirty-eight. Like Julius is that gun clean he repeated, the second time I'm so confused like damn how the hell he get from a light bid offer. Seemed like a wild ass case. Luckily, I didn't have no codefendants this shit wasn't adding up. In I just found out some fools was happy I got locked up. How anyone going to be happy that I get re arrested. I definitely knew the streets is over for me once I heard that.

Back to my lawyer I informed him the gun is clean I'm sure of that... I finally hit population and that's when I meet up with Collar Bone. Take you back real quick Collar Bone was coming up to Stegman n Bergen from time to time. Blood was sticking shit up in laying niggas down, he was suppose to get put on to the set. His ass got rearrested for a gun. It is why when I see him on population, I'm about to peace him as Brim. Started catching up on what was going on in this County. This is when I met Bless Fruit Town Brick City Brim 232 homie. After that Top shelf came on the tier. By the way Collar Bone from 464 Insane Mob Piru.

Top Shelf informing me and Collarbone how he went to a baby shower and saw a Crip. Him in another homie at the time waiting for the Crip to step outside so they can knock his head off. At this time we have an on-site with G Shine. Bless the Fruit Town Brick City Brim informing me that it's a G Shine on our tier. I walked right in blood room ask him wess bracken. Long story short blood said he isn't tripping I walked out the room. Around this time Monster Ru was found dead off the highway right by Northern State Prison.

Right after that Pencil Ru was killed. Pencil Ru was from Jersey City I believe he was shot up nine times. Monster Ru he was from Newark one of the first Mob Piru homies from the East Coast. Before it was 464 Insane Mob Pirus it was 662 Mob Piru. Monster Ru death started a vicious war within the Mob Pirus. Actually it was between 662 Mob and

464 Insane Mob Pirus right before that war kicked off though, everyone thought G-Shine had something to do with that it.

If so, all West Coast sets was going ride in the state of New Jersey. Reason being Monster Ru was a real one, let a long if something happen to a Westside homie. Every west coast set ride as one didn't matter. This new shit everyone on is real wack. Yet once the word got out G-Shine had nothing to do with it. All the west coast sets fell back. That war is apart of the reason. Damu Love is fucked up to this day. Before that vicious war the "Green Jackets" which is better known as the Bounty Hunter Bloods. 5 Line Bounty Hunters ,Outlaw Bounty Hunters and Lot Boys Bounty Hunter Bloods the war between them three sets was very vicious.

All over they only wanted one Bounty Hunter set in the state of New Jersey to take over. So many lives were lost between that vicious war all for nothing. It was all for nothing they all come from the same root of the tree. BHB.I.P to all the Fallen. Same goes for the Mob Piru homies. P.I.P to every falling that was killed. I'm probably one of the very few that miss how we used to all be.

Before Westside sets was killing off each other there were so much Damu love. You could pull up to any west side blood set it didn't matter what city you were in. Times has definitely change yeah that's just the beginning. At this time this buster ass nigga Los he's on a tier across from me. Before he gets on the tier Killa E in the homies inform blood about me. The fool Los like where blood at, homies like oh you going to know which one he is. Collar Bone, Top Shelf and Bless yell my name out through the tier, Los introduce himself including he has lieutenant.

Real quick this is at the time when we was all being lied to. You'll see I'm just warming up back to this snitch ass fool though. Not only he says he has lieutenant he kept talking about the other snitch that brought the shit from West Side South Central L.A. Don't get it twisted at that time we show respect. I'm speaking on far as Jersey City. We didn't do the extras which everybody else did though, keeping that fool name and our mouths in taking orders.

We did this shit on our own he just brought it out here. That's it and that's all. Back to this fool though, I ask blood what part of Jersey he from his reply was the Heights. I'm like how long you were home blood? Blood tell me at least 9- 10 months. I'm like 9 to 10 months, then why you wasn't coming on the hill? He try to say he didn't no where Fruit Town Brims were at. I'm like everybody knew where brims was at homie. By this time Collar Bone, Top Shelf just waiting for me to say I'm pop this fool.

I told blood I'm a find out. Around this time my youngest daughter mother is pregnant, that's Zy'onna I'm already watching a little baby growing up through pictures which is Julissa. In now I have to do the same with this one. At this time, I couldn't force on that I had three consecutive cases. 18 years with 85 second 25 years with 85 my last case that shit was in the air. I remember I went to court for punk ass drug case, with the homie Nightmare.

We both at court the Judge Cunningham I believe, bring up my 187 case from back then. Reason being because he looking at my new case but that has nothing to do with the case we here today for. Nightmare shake his head in like I told you stop fucking with them guns I knew right there they had it out for me I wasn't going home no time soon.

Nightmare was from Sex Money Murder. I calls out to the turf speaking with Mr. 187 blood confirmed he met Los and that was that. That was after I was gone though, he forget to mention Killa E told his ass he doesn't got no lieutenant. What Los do he fell the fuck back. He had Lieutenant though Killa E like man this our shit he didn't do shit.

One evening we get some new people on the tier. One of them were a 5 Deuce Hoover Crip, me ,Collar Bone and Heavy Head Ru. We had our backs turn Top Shelf was on it though, at the time Top Shelf didn't have no sneakers. So he ask for mines first asking what size I wore, I'm like a eight and a half.

Blood grab my sneakers next thing you know it, Top Shelf hit the Crip so hard. His head bounce off the window on the tier then stomp him. We all went back to our regular conversation. Me, Bless, Top Shelf, Collar Bone and Heavy Head Ru stood up late that night just beating down. Next day it was a homie named Sal Ru, Bix Bix Deuce Mob Piru he was from Newark. Blood had a cold ass Piru walk, especially with the cane.... he was yet to see my walk though....

Top Shelf done got release, same for Bless. In by the way Top Shelf is from Fruit Town Brims. Collar Bone started poppin off because they were taking too long to ship him out to go down state prison. After that I popped off on the Tech homie he was supposed to mention a statement in Killa E, BG case. Blood Money finally make it on the tier, he was from 464 Insane Mob Piru codefendants to Killa E, BG.

Blood was one of the first ones to be from Mob Piru, he had a nice Piru walk as well. Blood Money came back from downstate, telling me about the politics that was going on between Bix Bix Deuce Mob and 464 Insane Mob. Not my place to go any further the shit was just ridiculous. Blood on blood killings was getting out of hand, especially between the Pirus and the Bounty Hunters. Pirus against Pirus and Bounty Hunters against Bounty Hunters from that point on, Damu Love was shattered.

One night I had a visit Mr.187 a homie came with my youngest daughter mother, at the time she was pregnant. I'm bicking it with the homie first, the homie say to me nobody forget about you. My response was simple, I no nobody didn't forget about me I put too much work in. My rivals no. Honestly I was really upset because the only person I was hearing from was Mr.187. We spoke for a few more, then Mr. 187 came over. Mine you this is a glass window visit. I stood up we both bang brim towards the glass. Everyone looking at us like we was wild.

People just didn't understand to over stand how much we love this brim gang wholeheartedly. Blood was coming to see me every week with my youngest daughter mother. It was always hard for me to see Julissa, every time she seen my face always reach for me through the glass window yet I couldn't hold her at visit. One of my painful moments. That night I went straight to my cell ignored Blood Money and Heavy Head Ru lock my cell and just stared out the window.

Next morning the homies particularly Heavy Head Ru and Blood Money, thought my visit turn out bad. I let them know it was a good visit, it was just towards the end. Me and Blood Money getting ready for court though, meeting up with Killa E, 5 Bix, Baby Head Bussa, Jesse James, Smokey ton of other homies.

That particular day though, it was about 20-25 brim homies all locked up for the same shit. Cold cases and shootings. While we were in the bullpen come to find out one of the non affiliates was snitching on some homies case. Soon we found out we made that fool drink somebody piss and eat somebody shit. good old days. In our Hudson County Jail if you came in as a woman beater, rapist or child molester you was getting poked up and thrown off the second floor.

It happened countless times, it is the very reason they built that building that's across from the county jail. Last time I was at any Courthouse I was there for Killa E & B G. That day I was there for they court date, someone in the crowd says some slick shit. I immediately jumped up out my seat like what. Next thing you know it judge had Sheriff Department take all my information copy of my ID. Just in case something happened to somebody that was in that court room another time I was supposed to be there I got locked up the night before. My mama was there the first thing he asked where Gunna at. His daughter mama was there though, I was told she was upset because he never asked about her laughs....

Here Come The Feds

I was switch to another tier, baby max tier I was move to c500 West and the maxed tier was move to c500 East. So me and Killa E was right next door to each other. When I went outside to the yard this fool Los, inform me he got a letter from the snitch from out L.A stating about his status whatever that fool wrote it had to be about him crying. That he don't have lieutenant, when Killa E told him just fall back.

Being that it already was me and him in the county jail. Killa E never really said he didn't have it, that's when Killa E snapped in said you don't have shit now and told that snitch from L.A what it is. Don't you know Los wrote back on some crying shit he really wrote a letter saying the Jones Brothers just want to take over.

Blood was really a bitch, I see why he was put on to be the personal mascot for every beacon call. Remember he got put on down Northern State Prison gang unit before he was Fruit Town Brims he was G-Shine. Come to find out while he was in gang unit, he was being tied up he was getting his ass beat with a belt. In that snitch ass fool from L.A knew about all this shit which is a disgrace. Back to dick in the booty Los, somehow he ended up on my tier.

I've been waiting to get to this fool face to face, only reason homies was coming sideways Los force was only about status. We never gave a fuck about that it doesn't make you or break you. We bickin it one day Los get a letter from down Northern State Prison gang unit speaking about different statuses. I remember a time everybody in Essex County that was from Fruit Town Brick City Brim status was snatched because all they care about was status.

Blood from L.A added a new status call the general. I have to be honest when that happened I felt something wasn't right. I grew up listening to Damu Rida's The Relatives an Oyg Redrum 781. I never heard nothing about no damn status. At that time though what did we know. Anyway Los was saying I believe he got captain or Og, I'm not going to sit here in lie.

When everybody in the county heard that shit the building went haywire. Neighborhood 20 Bloods, 464 Insane Mob Pirus etc. like how the hell he get that before you and Killa E. Again status didn't exist to me I didn't get put on for that. You saying you a Og was a huge step but him come on. Another letter come down from Northern State Prison saying Los didn't have that. So, I'm setting up to give him a d p he ran and hit the glass for the correctional officer too open the main door to the tier. From that point on shit gets vicious with him.

After he checks in PC a lot of things started coming out about him. How he was going around saying that everybody was listening to him. He was the big homie of everyone, even telling the female guards he ran the county jail laughs.. Around this time my youngest daughter is born. My princess Zy'onna I remember having a funny feeling like she was born but I didn't know if she was born. Like I just knew a part of me was recreated and I was right. The sad part I seen Julissa take her first steps through glass window visit. I can't tell you enough how much that shit hurt.

It's a day I'm watching the max tier outside on the yard. Mostly everyone playing basketball either waiting to play next. The ball almost hit Killa E, Killa E grab that ball and the whole court froze. dead homies! Mind you everyone on that tier have hot ones(187). By this time my two cases was thrown out 2 supposedly hot ones lack of evidence. Now the Feds done picked up my damn case. Before I get into that, when I seen that shit what happened on the court I just smiled.

I found out the feds picked up my case for the first time unexpected court call. Its after 3 a.m. I'm like you have to be making a mistake I don't have court, the guard show me the list and there it was my name Julius Jones. Big black bold letters Federal Bureau, I just put my head down and shook my head. I just knew I wasn't seeing my daughter's no time soon.

Not on the outside anyway U.S Marshals pick me up and took me to downtown Newark Federal Building. Waiting for like over an hour in find out I'm at the wrong Federal Building. So now we hit the highway and we headed to Trenton New Jersey a bigger Federal Building. As I walk in yet not moving much, due to the shackles on my ankles as well my wrist I'm moving like an inch at a time.

Right before, I get to where the cells are at you see fools sitting outside they cells eating. Without any shackles on they ankles, definitely not on they wrist. They all eating McDonald's, Dunkin Donuts even Popeye's I mean these fools are really eating this shit, sitting right next to a big ass pool table. I'm saying to myself where the hell do they do that at.

As, I'm sitting in the cell waiting to be arraigned, federal agent happened to stop by and notice how I was just amazed what they were over there eating. Mind you this all new to me, from doing time in state prison even more so federal. You hear all the time about older men doing federal time but yet you never hear them speak about what goes on. I see why most of them are snitches they damn self. So the agent get straight to the point said straight up, you can have whatever you want long as you cooperate or you going to be working for us in just walked away. I'm like damn clean cut and dry this how they playing.

I get inside that federal court room the judge is just a statue compared to the prosecutor, the prosecutor handles everything while the judge just agree to it or not. Prosecutor inform me on my charges right before I left I heard the prosecutor asked he's sure he don't want to corroborate or work for us. I just told the federal agents they can escort me out now there's nothing else to discuss.

As we leaving out the parking lot there's a huge crowd of young teenagers at the end of the corner. A few of them have some flags hanging out they back pocket, federal agent the driver ask me if I have anything to say to these young teens. All I said was if you have some skills, force on that the feds are coming. It was a nice long ride back, one of many I was going to be taken. I just knew I was going to at least going to be doing ten years out of my daughters lives at that. I finally get back to the county jail Hudson County.

Killa E patiently waiting to find out what is going on, I'm just like they got me. He asked did they bring up his case. I'm like not yet, his reaction was surprising he like what you mean not yet. I'm like the way they was talking like they just putting pieces together, I don't know what it is. At this time Killa E, B G case was looking great their wasn't no offers or witnesses. Months later though I received my presentence report from the feds called PSI.

As I'm reading it, it has my set Fruit Town Brims from South Central L.A and also I have 4 confidential informants. They knew that night that I got rearrested I was already coming down Arlington Park. The Federal Gang Unit knew what type of shirt I had on in everything, the shirt sticks out the most to me. I just got that shirt made the same day I was rearrested I had picked it up that morning cold game! It was homies with me that morning to when I picked up my shirt. They also got shirts made I was the only one target though.

The Feds even said they knew what type of gun I like using and carrying…talk about betrayal shit I was beyond hurt….

Getting Sentence

PSI isn't nothing more than a summary of your case, of what they have so far. It is not paperwork I repeat it is not paperwork. They give you a federal chart and all of that, the federal chart is about how many months which adds up to years depending on your background. Let's say you did three prison bids, each prison bid is 3 points which give you a total of 9 points. It don't have nothing to do with your actually charge. Let's say you didn't complete probation that's an extra point, now if you did complete probation then it remains 0. In a sense that's double jeopardy it doesn't have nothing to do with your case that you're being charge with.

Them points alone gives you months and again it don't have nothing to do with your actually charge. Federal Bureau play a whole different league in by this time we about to pop correctional officer he was pretending he was real tough, all because he claims some blood on the streets of East Orange New Jersey killed his brother. So he felt the right to use his authority, by not allowing us to watch TV or go out on the rec yard and not giving us our canteen. Me Heavy Head Ru and Sex Money Murder homie surrounded his ass he immediately called for backup. We had gang task force within our County Jail. It was a Spanish woman and a dark skinned woman she was from Newark the dark skin women. Spanish women was from Jersey City.

They were handling all gang members especially that had names. They both say in front of everybody how you doing Mr. Gunna, you really be keeping this building and this tier interesting. A real live wire in a sense its like they intrigued by it. I'd be lying though, if I caught they asses outside of this county I would have dick both of their asses down. Spanish one had long hair I can see myself gripping that shit from behind and the chocolate one oh man the darker the sweeter the juice. The whole time the correctional officer male he just quiet and looking goofy. In as the gang task force women walk away, they say it loud enough for me and the homies can hear them. Girl and he got locks. I say about like over a month later Los reappears like jack in the box he still in PC though.

He had the nerve to threaten a homie though, about how he going catch the homie because he the one that hit the bubble ran and checked in PC. The homie tells me and I asked him what he said, his response was like nah I wasn't talking to you homie. I'm like you brazy as hell, come out of PC then if you feel that way. Blood kept it quiet after that, little do anybody know that was a starting point on him getting his revenge on everybody and more. By this time Fruit Town Fresh is on the same tier as me, Big Sha in Spazz are on d-unit. Spazz popping off Big Sha always trying to calm him down. It was a day I was out in the yard bickin it with Big Sha he was still on his unit though. In "Hudson County Jail" we speak sign language with our hands. This really our first introduction on speaking, something happened on his tier.

 I'm like we catch them fools on a rebound homie and leave their asses. It was actually small that was just my hot headed ass at that time. Big Sha was like fools said you love playing with them guns. My reply was like, I remember you in action. You didn't see me though, it was on the Dwight n Jackson you clear that shit and board day. Then Fruit Town Fresh got my attention, like that buster Los out of PC he on the tier with Saleem. Fruit Town Fresh tell the fool Saleem to pop that buster Los, he shouldn't have to tell him because everybody should know what to do. All Saleem kept saying that he going to do it in never got done. The next morning Los disappears, Saleem claims he didn't know he was going to court out Essex County. It never happened because they were buddy buddy down Northern State Prison, as well they both were G Shine before being from Fruit Town Brims.

I get a visit during the day by my youngest daughter mother. I see my baby girl for the first time, she look just like me and my sister Twin Twin. I inform my daughter mother it's going to be awhile before I get out. Her response was like at least you got them 2 cases out the way, I say you damn right. The next morning I get a visit from my sister Erica she informed me she originally came to get Ron G fat ass out. So she like he going to have sit till I finished with my visit. The visit was an hour. After the visit later on that day I had got a letter and a lot of pictures from Juelz, surprisingly he been writing me the second I got locked up consistently.

Truthfully I never would have thought he would have, he mention in the letter on my sentencing day he was going to be there. By this time instead of releasing Killa E, B G everyone else because the state didn't have no evidence. Still no offer no witnesses no nothing they decide to push their case to the feds. I took 11 years in the feds and I was about to get sentence. On my sentencing day for the state I had a probation violation which was running concurrent with my federal case. In what do you know my judge Mr. Cunningham, when he seen my face his exact words was. I really was trying to put you away for a long time. The next time I see your face you automatically going to get life. Juelz brought my oldest daughter Princess, came along with Julissa mother.

Julissa was knocked out, when Princess heard the word life. She broke down and cried, that's when the judge at least allow me 20 minutes in the conference room with my daughters. Princess was holding me so tight, it hurt her even more that my wrist was shackle with cuff, I couldn't hold her back tight. She broke down even more as Princess holding me crying, I'm not going to get the chance to experience with Julissa what I experienced with Princess. Watching movies together, help her take a bath, tuck her in at night and read her bedtime stories. My federal charge was some fake gang bangin shit with a gun. I saw my daughter Zy'onna in her mama along with Mr.187. Zy'onna mama all she said was hurry back home. We are outside the courtroom and let me speak to Mr. 187 in Zy'onna mama for 5 minutes. Mr.187 like keep it brimish, my reply isn't no question.

I starred at my daughter Zy'onna for the next 2 minutes kiss her on her forehead U S Marshals took me. Now that I'm sentence I'm ready to go to get this shit over with, when you gang bangin theirs all types of different levels with this shit. You have the streets the county and prisons your track record to the next level to becoming a rep ute able. Back at the county I call my mama, to inform her about my sentencing. She took a deep breath, took it all in now she has to worry about her youngest son. Killa E also watching his daughter grow up through pictures. Best believe I'm still trying to figure out who is the four continental informants.

For those that don't know, that mean they working only thing that saved me their wasn't no wiretaps. I definitely would have been done I get one more visit, from my mama just saying. Keep remaining strong like I know you are, I'm glad you didn't give up. In what she meant by that is this when I had them other two cases for them hot ones, I was just going to give up I didn't give a fuck. Then she said to me one thing she always loved about me I never gave up on anything I was involved in that's all I needed to hear. My mama was a true definition of a gem, after all this shit her son's put her through she still kept it together. Left visit Fruit Town Fresh went to lockup, for popping somebody ass. Homies was beating down about the streets, and how they did things on they blocks. To me they were moving carelessly even to the point, letting the addicts disrespect the residence.

So, I brought up a time about my relative Taisha, this was back then when she was living on Stegman n Bergen in the building actually where the Fruit Town Brims be at. She was stressing to me how the drug addicts was always getting high in front of the kids and having sex in front of her door late at night. So one night she told me exactly where they always be at, I waited until there were all together. All you have to do is make a example out of one of them. Soon I seen him i pistol-whipped him twice and pushed him down the stairs. Grab him up put the pistol in his mouth. Now I'm speaking to him I'm looking at the group from now on nobody get high in front of no kids nor residence. You protect the residents they protect you, it's all about respect. In that particular building there were two ways to come in and out.

I always use that to my advantage, if I served you on one side 5 minutes later I had you leave out the other door vice versa. I never did anything in front of no kids or residence. It is why when the feds try to get the residents to speak badly about me they did the opposite. That alone will save you to get less time most importantly that's just in me isn't that being blood is all about? Protecting the community to the best of your ability Julius Jones pack up you getting shipped out to go downstate.

Welcome To Yardville

I was on the road headed straight to craft which is out Trenton New Jersey craft is a place where you get sent to, find out the destination what prison you going to. I met some Bounty Hunters they were from 5 Line, they were really on they hunter shit. All four were from Paterson New Jersey, I also met some Neighborhood Pirus. Sex Money Murder and G Shine was killing off each other and a medical area. It was a major war going on outside Trenton New Jersey, that war started because one person flip to another set.

It couldn't get no wilder Tech gang got involved. There were so many killings going on, they started having they homies wakes at the same place. Things were getting out of hand at the funeral homes as well Bounty Hunter Bloods were still going at it as well too. I get my destination I'm headed to Yardville State Prison. Getting on that white bus shackled with somebody else side by side, I was ready to get off the bus already he was annoying. There were a lot of wars going on, especially about Monster Ru P.I.P a lot of shooting and killings going back and forth, homies getting time left and right. Quite a few faces looking nervous as hell, headed down state.

This is my very first time going to prison. The older heads in people in general talked about prison like it was the right to passage. Well I'm here to tell you different, the whole time I was in prison I felt like a loser. You'll see isn't nothing gangster about being in prison especially when you have mouths depending on you. Getting off the bus we inside the building, going to the receptionist.

Immediately treated like nothing take off your clothes been over cough open your mouth flip your tongue and spread your ass cheeks then cough again. Then Co(Correctional officer) designate you to a housing unit. Before I get to my actually housing unit, was sent to a holding tier. Then I ran into a homie, at least I thought he was still Fruit Town Brims.

Blood flip to another set Sex Money Murder talking about nobody write him or do anything for him I still ask him.

That's the reason why you flipped so who was to say you wouldn't do that in the interrogation room. Nobody owe us nothing, I said I feel some type of way yeah I never thought about flipping to any other set. I knew what I signed up for. I hit him with this, how you speaking about loyalty when you not even loyal to yourself. Forget all that though, you coming back to Fruit Town Brims or you already know what it is. It was two Fruit Town Brick City Brim homies, mention to me just give them the call.

Blood decide to come back to Fruit Town Brim damn near everybody down Yardville is from different sets. During this time Duke boys transition to 793 Beven Gang. Duke Boys were actually Tech gang also but riding the 5 they had what you call lineups. You had head busser 2 they were also Tech gang another lineup. You had Gambino line, Stacks line they were Sex Money Murder I can't begin to say all the lines, it were so many of them. I forget the G Shine lines but they were definitely getting it bracken. Double ii Bloods 235 ,Elm Street Piru, Outlaw 20s Bloods, Neighborhood 20s Bloods 27blk and 29blk. Let me break it down real quick, you see L.A sets we bang streets and blocks being in L.A where ever you live at if you was put on to a set, that's what you bang.

This isn't a game this is a culture, a culture that been lasting for over five decades. You have kid's that are born in it, it's not a fab being a blood has nothing to do with status. Gang bangin is about recognition and never forgetting the dead. It's a generation thing, your generation is your generation nobody can take it from you. What you do from day to day week to week month to month and year to year. That what determines on who you are as a Blood, Piru or Brim. Nobody can give you a Og status, for you to even be considered and Og you had to be put on at least in the 80s. At least no later than 85- 86. To be a Triple Og if you wasn't no founder co-founder or there from the beginning, you definitely not know Triple Og. Second generation towards the mid late 70s very early 80s.

Back to so many sets you had Cedar Block Pirus, 135 Pirus, 464 Insane Mob Piru, Lost Boys Bounty Hunter Bloods, Fruit Town Brick City Brims 232 and oh Lacey from G Shine his lineup was definitely getting it bracken. In a host of other sets. Far as West Coast sets Fruit Town Brims 36th Street, Fruit Town Brick City Brims, 464 Insane Mob Piru and Double ii Bloods 235 were the deepest other sets had a nice little number it wasn't a movement though. They were still about they business. When I go to the gym for wreck one of the Sex Money Murder big homies approach me with respect, his name is Poppy blood from Jersey City.

Blood was busting his gun behind that Sex Money Murder it was about the homie that was once Brim went to Sex Money Murder, then came back to Fruit Town Brims. Let me break it down how Jersey do real quick. You see being that actuality like I said previously that 5 doesn't exist being a blood. Which represent People Nation another culture which derives from Chicago gangs. In has nothing to do with L.A culture the same goes for the six point star that's called Folk Nation which you got some Crips saying they are 6 point star people really need to know they history. If you don't know what you're being a part of you are a born follower.

So back to what I was saying, being that anybody that was riding the 5, it was bool you getting put on to a west coast set.

A west coast set couldn't go to, a east coast set that meant war. So Poppy like blood went back to Fruit Town Brim huh I'm like fa'sho. He definitely said he knew he wasn't going to stay Sex Money Murder yet was it bool if anybody felt they wanted to shoot the fade. I told blood like he already said he with that. Poppy was like he told his homies he was going to bick it with me, also informed them that a homie from a west side set couldn't go to a eastside set. In all reality during that time we were lace wrong. We just didn't know that all that shit was goofy.

 I was even more wrong for doing that in the first place, why would I want somebody back when he already showed he was disloyal. You definitely learn from experience and mistakes or you will drown. Poppy like you don't have to stay over here you can fuck with me and the homies. I replied I'm not with the fake shit blood, our set's don't even like each other if this were on the streets we wouldn't be talking. We always had respect for one another but your homies you already know. Whoever want that fade though we could definitely line it up BRIM GANG....

Get back to the unit they take me to south house, when I get to south house word get backs to me that the homie that switch back to Fruit Town Brim checked in PC. The officers on the unit they took who they wanted to take down stairs and we walked upstairs, first thing they said out their mouth if you are blood and your fake, you not about that gang life, in you pretended to be tough you not who you say you are let us know now. Once you go in the back either sides because it was four different parts of the unit.

Whatever happens back there happens until they finish with you and throw your body towards the gate we not coming back there to get nobody. Man it was like seven people hit PC laughs the first homie I saw was Money, Money was from Lexington. Lexington is a block in Jersey City a well-known getting money block at one point. Money was put on to 464 Insane Mob Piru he was locked up for his second hot one doing 5 years. He get me moved in the room with him. Not only it was a west side thing we knew each other from the streets. Then I met Luda he was from Lot Boys Bounty Hunter Bloods. Blood was really holding that shit down, then the young homie named Doughboy from Lakewood he was put on to Fruit Town Brims 36th Street.

The rest was east side sets, I'm from the era where it was west against east. I didn't deal with them like that let alone ever shake their hands. It just what it is because on the streets it was on site. Don't let nobody fool you in tell you different, it was west side the best side the only side that ride. Anybody that was pushing a west coast set that was our saying. Those that were riding the 5, they will say east side is the beast side.

One night I see the homie Doughboy walking with some shower slippers on his feet, I immediately told blood you never walk around with shower slippers on your feet. No bloods don't we got to be on point.

Even when walking to the shower you have your boots or sneakers on. Any blood that have to take a shower let a homie no. A homie will walk you to the shower and stand guard, this was being done in my county jail. They definitely wasn't doing that until I got to Yardville, only us west side bloods was doing that far as on my tier. Money was on his way about to go home, he left me a nice amount of canteen food. At the time I had nothing really positive to say, I was fully gang banged out. I just said stay dangerous Big Bs too tall Ps. If you notice I haven't mentioned no Crips, there weren't any Crip sets on population. If they were they haven't made it known, from time to time one will get caught and pop on. They would be deep down Annandale Prison and Southern State Prison during that time 03 04 05 and 06 them years.

There were some MS 13s and they were deep some Latin Kings and Netas. The Latin Kings were definitely in directly connected to Chicago same as the MS 13s was connected to L.A. Big differences between New York and New Jersey Latin Kings in New York a lined themselves with the east coast bloods in New York that started on Rikers Island now in the state of New Jersey Latin Kings, Sex Money Murder, G shine and Tech gang they would war with one another. Even in Jersey City Latin Kings, Sex Money Murder be going at it, it's been a couple of murders happen between one another. In Jersey we stick to the script it's the reason we take so much pride in this gang shit.

I go to the receptionist to get my photo ID I see my gangster Collar Bone from 464 Insane Mob Piru, blood like Wess Mobbin Gunna my reply was like I'm brimtainin keeping it brimish. Blood was being shipped out Collar Bone was like I'm poppin all Double ii niggas I'm not feeling them niggas or them Newark niggas they think they better than us(Jersey City). Collar Bone was getting shipped out because he was popping all they asses. They were taking him as we walking past one another I'm like Su Woop business. Later on that night go to rec to the gym, this when I met Hem, Bishop and Babe B G they all was from Fruit Town Brick City Brim 232 we introduce each other at first me and Babe B G got off to a rocky start.

I remember Collar Bone pacifically saying these Newark fools really think they better then Jersey City. He was going on and on about the history and how everything he was saying was on point, I'm like blood all that shit wrong then Bishop jumped in and try to back him up. Confident as I am I repeated that shit is wrong. You know in this gang world pride and ego be at its highest peak, nevertheless it didn't matter to me. That shit is all wrong tension was in the air throughout the night at the gym. This is when I met Reek Hood from Jersey City he was Neighborhood Rollin 20 Bloods I believe 29th block. We bickin it the rest of the night.

Me and the Fruit Town Brick City Brim homies we were on different tiers yet we were on the same housing unit. I'm speaking to the young homie Doughboy his reply was like they probably jealous because you corrected them. At this time Bishop has sergeant, our housing unit get raided. We all ended up back at the gym, that's when everything comes out they did a little background check on me like why you aren't saying you were lieutenant. My reply locking eyes with each one of them, what status have to do with being a brim we all suppose to up lift one another up especially if we was inform miss information.

Not going back and forth who's wrong who's right why you think I left it alone. If I no I'm right I'm not debating with nobody, then it just means I'm doubting myself. Little did I know that clown from L.A misled all of us. After that we all became tight, I believe they respected me more because I wasn't on no status shit. Damn near everyone else that's all they care about for real for real. This around the time I started really seeing this status shit was divide in conquer. I've never experienced nothing like this, everything was about Damu Love on the streets and prison though the average conversation was about what you got an who gave it to who.

I can honestly say I never got caught up and none of that. So we at the gym Babe B G brought up an interesting situation, he was speaking on about his celli. His celli said if you get into anything he would ride with him, I say to Babe B G that's the business. As we was talking his celli walked towards our direction, as he's walking blood point to him and I'm like he brim. Baby B G like no he not, and I say I know blood personally we went to the same grammar school. I'm like blood got put on by Killa E, you mean to tell me blood didn't let you know that he was Fruit Town Brim. Baby B G was just shock. I had Babe B G call him over, I'm like blood you didn't tell the homie that you brim, the homie response was I don't deal with everybody like that.

I'm like what, that's like you're denying that you're brim. It doesn't matter if you deal with everyone or not you don't never deny you Brim. Never. I asked the homie are you ashamed, his reply was no my reply was your actions speak volumes. I turned to blood Babe B G he have to get DP blood on brim. Making Jersey City Brims look bad in shit, don't get it twisted brim is brim but blood listen. When you get put on by somebody especially a rider, you not only make yourself look bad you make the person that put you on bad even more I was mad as shit. After that I didn't have shit else to say to blood. Sometime in the afternoon days later, Luda from Lot Boys Bounty Hunter Bloods was informing me about somebody from New Brunswick, New Jersey saying he wanted to get put on to Bounty Hunters.

Ask about my input on it, myself I was curious to know why he waited till he get locked up to decide to get put on. So, I say to Luda didn't you say his best friend from Neighborhood 20 Bloods. So if he claimed that's his best friend why would he want to get put on to Bounty Hunter and he don't even know you. Most importantly getting put on in jail that shit isn't official. Anybody can have the heart to get put on in prison, to see where somebody at get put on the streets. The correct in only way you see if anyone really with this shit being active. I said me personally I wouldn't do it, Luda reply was he was on the same shit he just respected my opinion. I say okay your Ludacris looking ass laughs (blood definitely look just like him) I used to ride blood about that all the time.

That same night I decided to have a little fun, I tell the young homie Doughboy when that non-affiliated scream out for the shower first say you got that shit. I just want to see how he going to react. The non-affiliated is the same one that wanted to get put on to Bounty Hunter Bloods. It just like I thought he back down, Doughboy said shower after him he told him he was going first. Non affiliated going to say you got it, cold buster. You won't believe the next day, non affiliated tried to get put on by me, he like I've never heard of Fruit Town Brim before. I got to the conclusion he was really a groupie, I'm like blood wasn't you trying to get put on to Bounty Hunter Bloods now you coming at me. He has the puzzle look, like us Damus don't talk or something.

I just walked away from him. Couple of days go by, this non-affiliated says bloods from other sets, say don't get put on by Gunna he going to have you going around killing Crips. That night he got put on to Sex Money Murder. About two months later some wild shit happen on another housing unit. A Sex Money Murder homie kept stealing from a MS 13, going in his locker. The MS 13 inform the Sex Money Murder homies that they homie kept stealing from him, Sex Money Murder homies told MS 13s that they would take care of their homie. It never happened so, one very early morning MS 13 wakes up about 4 a.m. Sex

Money Murder homie sleeps above the MS 13 so he waits for the Sex Money Murder homie to wake up, once the Sex Money Murder homie seen that long shank in the MS 13 hand he try to run.

MS 13 grab him so quick, wrapped his arm around the Sex Money Murder body was trying to slit his throat from one end to the next. He moved his neck so it went up towards his head. Then the MS 13 started jigging the shank in and out the Sex Money Murder stomach. I don't even know if he made it or not. I do know this, all them Sex Money Murder homies throughout the whole prison was acting like they didn't no who did that shit. In right after that MS 13 started popping off, every Sex Money Murder housing unit. All this was taking place because somebody was stealing out someone locker. Homies going back and forth what should be done what shouldn't be done. Me Babe BG and Bishop were like that's what his ass gets for stealing.

Not too long after that some foul shit happen. Three black high school kids, were killed in Irvington New Jersey by MS 13s. MS 13s talking about for they initiation the fourth kid survive, all four kids were lined up against the wall in the schoolyard. Later that night we were all in the gym, every blood in the prison of Yardville decided to ride on MS 13s. It was the principal that they were innocent, they had no gang ties something has to be done about that shit. Next day for hours it became bloody in every population. I Almost get stabbed in the head, like I said before them MS 13s were deep. We were going so hard for days that shit went on completely lockdown. Right before count down every night we were only allow 45 minutes to make something to eat or shower. Wasn't allowed no canteen, so if you didn't have no food you was eating what they were giving you or you wasn't going to eat nothing. For breakfast and lunch they were only giving you a boiled egg and jello. They had to give you a hot meal once a night though. A very few months later I was packing up next stop Northern State Prison....

Finally Northern State Prison

I believe it was a very early Wednesday morning, that I was called over the loudspeaker at Yardville Julius Jones get ready to go to Northern State Prison. Northern State Prison is in Newark New Jersey, everyone has to understand to over stand during this time which was 2006. Northern State Prison was the Mecca, for anybody claiming they were somebody that's where you wanted to be at. During this time gang unit was down Northern State Prison, which started the end of 1999 or beginning of 2000. Truthfully because of the snitch from L.A....

It's about over an hour drive or so, before we get there. Honestly, I was anxious to get there, just to see what this shit was about. Don't get it twisted though, they were a lot of names that were somebody that didn't make it. When we finally get there, go through the same process and the receptionist area. Strip off all your clothes, lift each feet up, squat, turn around and bend over, spread your ass cheek and cough, turn back around and open your mouth, lift your tongue up. Now get dressed. Shit was beyond humiliated, each time I did that I felt less than a man. That was the point though, the system designed it like that. We walking to the compound everyone outside on each housing unit, the side I'm walking on is called Compton.

I'm g strolling through compound, all types of homies throwing up they sets to see what set I'm from. I immediately reply back throwing up 36th Street and banging Brim. Hell of homies started throwing up the W 4 West Side. We reach A1 housing unit, which is a holding unit your held there before going to another housing unit. When I walk through the tier, a Fruit Town Brick City Brim 232 homie name Dutch spotted me. He knew I was Brim the way I wore my Skull hat that they gave me in reception, I had it bent cock to the side. Dutch greeting me like wess Brimin, I reply brim gang or don't bang. He just smile like all the time homie. It's about time for lunch, so our unit walk to the next unit and that's when the Brim homie Dutch started stacking throwing up Brim.

A Dove homie from 27th block, Doves are another term for Neighborhood Rollin 20 Bloods he threw up Neighborhood and 7 down. I threw up 36th Street bent my hat then threw up brim. During these times this how we did it, the mighty Brims shit back then we were most hated. The smallest yet the loudest, during these times we were very vicious. Nobody can't say anything different. Me in the Brim homie Dutch by the way this Dutch is dark skin, hit the yard. The first Brim homie I met from another housing unit, his name was Mister Head Bussa he was Fruit Town Brick City Brim. Blood ask me what other spot I just came from, my reply was Yardville.

He brought up Hem & Bishop saying they riders, I told blood they definitely down for Brim. We was on the same housing unit just on different tiers. I told him I'm Gunna Fruit Town Brim homie, his reply was oh you the homie Gunna. Yeah the homies said that you were down, we were expecting you to be taller and bigger. I met a couple of other homies then I seen my relative Black, we haven't seen each other since he caught his hot one he was from Sex Money Murder his hands is license. We spoke on a the few relatives, Grunt, Snoop in Kaka. Kaka is Sex Money Murder as well just speaking on family time, how so many of us and our family is behind the wall. As well how we use to meet up on Armstrong and ocean.

Then we spoke on our relative Jarvis, how he did someone dirty. We spoke a few more then he sent me some canteen, till my property came. During these times mandatory paperwork was check, especially when you had a name. By time your name reach the compound your background was already checked. Then my gangster B G came outside, B G that's Fruit Town Brim 36th Street. Me and B G actually were on the streets together, our Brimin were way different. There's a big difference between being put on in prison, getting put on the streets and then a rider. When you out there frontline 24/7, it's the way you move, your stance, your militant you're aura. You automatically stood out truth be told already sense jealousy.

Especially the way B G reacted when he seen me, you can tell he really fuck with me. Now you actually got two Brims down Northern State Prison was locked up behind the set. A lot of Brims were prison Bloods, just like a lot of other sets. I always show respect as a man, when it came to this Brimin though a lot of these fools can't speak my language. That's the part B G was talking about, on his housing unit they were concerned just about status. We both like a lot of homies think this shit a game. By the way at Northern State it was lockdown 23 and 1, pick and choose rec out side for a hour or rec in the gym for hour.

A few days later me and B G we bickin it, B G let me know all the brim homies on his housing unit asked about me. B G inform everyone that I was a head Bussa I was the main one pressing the line, alongside Mr.187. This during my time I was out there, before that it was B G and Killa E. Back in our time Paterson and Jersey City were one. Me and B G reminiscing like fools just don't know. I get called over the loud speaker the following morning, Julius Jones you getting moved. B G was still trying to get me to come on his unit. I was getting moved to the other side, which we called the Jungles.

Like the movie on Training Day Baldwin Village the Jays.... I get sent to F housing unit. I met a homie from Paterson yet he flipped so, theirs no need to mention his name. At that time he was the only homie on that tier though. He was going home like another two or three days or something like that. A Brim homie from Jersey City heard I was over there, Blood walk to my tier look who it was Big L Brim. Big L Brim was the tier rep for his side, so his ass be moving around. We haven't seen each other since like 2000, for short little while we went to the same grammar school together. We bickin it up dating each other what is going on. Big L Brim and Jesse James ran the housing unit. Big L Brim had Fruit Town and Jesse James had Brick City, before Big L Brim caught his hot one case he was a real problem on the streets.

We go outside and meet up with Jesse James again, at first Blood going sit there like he didn't remember me. Homies be acting real different when they around their own backyard. He was definitely one of them, Blood stay going to court in my County Jail. He only built conversations with me and Killa E. Anyway though I meet 187, Meat, Murder, Bad Ass, Boopdaville, Loyalty, V Brim a few other homies from Newark they were all Fruit Town Brick City Brim 232. Then the Fruit Town Brim 36th Street homies Beefy from Elizabeth New Jersey, Tye Brim and Chuck Taylor both from Camden New Jersey no need to mention the other homies they either turned out bad or some more shit. Oh the homie Taliban from Newark.

At first me Loyalty and 187 instantly bump heads, like they were trying to tell me and Fruit Town Brim homies what to do. You see homies out Newark they don't say Fruit Town Brick City Brims, they just say Brick City Brim, I kept shit the original way that's how it started. It was very few words being exchanged, then Big L Brim, Jesse James and the rest of the homies got in between. They like this Brick City, I'm like this apples peaches and plums wess bracken.

Come to find out they were on some jealous shit because Jersey City was getting the same respect as Newark. Most importantly it started coming out a lot homies from Newark was hating on Killa E status. Yet a lot of homies from Newark really show respect and Brim love, later on both of the homies turned out to be bool. Me and the homie Beefy used to build all the time, as well Chuck Taylor and Boopdaville. Boopdaville was from East Orange New Jersey they some down ass homies, so is 187. Taliban inform me Murder Man Cee his brother, said calm my hotheaded ass down. Murder Man Cee is a rider, at that time he was down Rahway State Prison.

As I was down North State Prison I was lacing a lot of homies. Besides being outside for a hour or in the gym, Big L Brim use to bick it with me everyday. One day Killa Reek was snatching certain fools status, that's all fool's were hitting him for. It was about like 2 or 3 months later though, it was a situation with Beefy. I forget what the Brim homie said what to him, all I know it was on some oppression shit. Long story short I back him up, we in the yard and I said you popping I'm popping to. From that point on we was tight as hell. A little after that B G making on our side, he didn't like it on our side. His exact words were there is no love between Brims, everyone wanted to be a chief. He even said he had a situation with a Brim homie from Newark. Again no disrespect it's not all Newark homies, during this time though. A lot of homies that were in prison, definitely acting like they were better than everybody else from anywhere else. Little did we know as a whole our shit were going to crash. By this time No Exit make it down Northern State Prison and E Trills from Fruit Town Brick City Brim 2007. Me and E Trills were down Yardville together, Blood was popping off down the Ville he a original from Newark same as Boopdaville, Bishop, Hem an as well being out Camden Chuck Taylor another 187 far as being what cities their were from when Brim started.

By this time I use to be building with Mr. Mobster , Hazy Ru and B O they all were 464 Insane Mob Piru in a Bounty Hunter homie from New Brunswick New Jersey he was Lot Boys. The home of all Bounty Hunter Bloods, when it come to Jersey. If you not on your Bounty Hunter shit don't go to New Brunswick. Blood had cK blasted right under his left eye, I know his real name is Kenneth. That were my gangster, me him Mr. Mobster used to always listen to Ol English song by The Game. Damu Rida's Tru Flue Killer, Ygb's Are The Braziest, Bangin on Wax Mafia Lane, Can't Stop, Won't Stop etc. you know we were reminiscing I informed them the night I got rearrested me and Mr. 187 we weren't supposed to be in Jersey City that night.

I was paying for both of our round trip tickets to L.A dead homies. Something came up so I pushed the date back, I believe it was something with his job. Oh by the way yes we both is working, this what I mean a lot of homies was just out there just to be out there. At this time though, me and Mr. 187 our mentality was very different though. We were going out there to not only meet the homies, to show them how Jersey do it though on Westside Brims. Like I said before my time was very different, so just imagine if we would have went out there back then. I'm let everybody see what I'm talking about.

Sex Money Murder war started popping off, it was between what they call lineups within they own set. Straight dumb shit, all over one lineup thinking they better than the other. Truthfully most of their wars down Northern State Prison were at each other within their own sets. Us west side bloods we used to always trip over that shit, like how you feel comfortable being that set, sad part west side bloods the same way now. After that the Beven homies in Latin King's started popping off in knifing each other. Latin Kings got the best of them that day, the homie Reckless he was Head Bussa he's from Newark blood was a real rider.

He press the issue about that shit, like how no other homies that were Tech gang ride with them. Honestly though Duke Boys in Head Bussa never got a long, Reckless thing were we black they got to go. After the doors popped Beven got they get back and a real way. Then it popped off three more times in a row. Now we on complete shutdown. Each cell hold two people, every three rooms we had 10 minutes for shower mind you there were only one shower hose. So it's three grown men sharing one shower hose, going back and forth to watch themselves without any hot water, after that lockdown. Neighborhood 20 Bloods 27 block & 29 block against Sex Money Murder 252. By this time it's a homie name Attica and So Good they both were Neighborhood 20 Bloods 27 block.

Attica from Newark and So Good was from East Orange. That war started over a cell phone, the homie Attica ask to used the Sex Money Murder homie cell phone, the homie Attica said he not giving that shit back. Sex Money Murder homies tell blood he got a certain day and time to give the phone back. That very next morning, blood smoking a cigarette in the corner, as soon as he finished spoken that cigarette, Attica went straight at blood knifed him in his eye and pull that shit out. During this time Reek Hood from Jersey City was down Northern State Prison 2 the same Reek Hood I left down Yardville. At this time there wasn't that many Neighborhood 20 Bloods.

Sex Money Murder homies popped off Reek Hood and So Good they didn't get the best of them though because they both were prepared. None of the west side sets didn't like that shit. So we all started popping off and knifing. The shit was already planned, longs they ride for themselves we all was following. Don't get it twisted we had our situations, when it came to a west side homie it was on in bracken. A little after that the homie HBo from Paterson New Jersey came down on the tier with Big L Brim, No Exit was on my line far as my cell we can speak to each other through the vent. I called out to the streets, my youngest daughter mother she tells me Dead Wrong got shot twice in the head and Killa another Fruit Town Brim homie got shot in the eye and hip.

First thing I asked do they know who did that shit, her reply was the person that did it got killed right after he shot Killa in the eye and Dead Wrong twice in the head. I was so hot I just hung up, I told No Exit. I didn't want to talk to nobody else for the rest of that night. We were finally allowed to go to rec at the gym, I was reminiscing to No Exit. The last time I saw Dead Wrong was in the county jail, we see each other he was on D100 pod. His last words to me were, I love you blood keep holding that shit up. Another homie that was on his way in the music industry.

From that situation on Brims started going up out in streets. One day my mama brought Julissa to come and see me, she kept staring at me like she couldn't believe she were seeing her daddy physically. She grab my locks and started playing in my locks, look at me dead in the eyes I need you and want you to come home Daddy. I fought back the tears and it shattered me. I couldn't even say anything, I just held her tight. I speak about it in Invincible Tears Vol 1. and a lot of other thing's. I remember a time Juelz flew from ATL to come and see me.

Yeah like I said Blood was really by my side. Right after that Brims and Piru had a big ass war, Mob Piru homies killed Hood from Fruit Town Brick City Brim. This was actually the first time wars on the streets spread in the prisons. When they killed blood, our performance was marvelous, we showed our asses on the streets. Sad part though we all Bloods. It was going down so much, during visiting hours in front of people family members and kids. I believe two people got paralyzed. After we get off lockdown for like a month in two weeks. Me and No Exit started reminiscing again, Beefy and Taliban is by us. He like remember that time we were down Arlington Park one night when Harlem 30 Crips ride through being disrespectful.

I'm like yeah do I remember, I was talking to a female on the side block mostly everybody forgot I was even in that area. As soon I heard that shit they were screaming that shit out the sunroof fuck Brims this Harlem 30s Crips. I'm running behind the car while dumping at it. I'm like by then you had your second one (hot one). We both like the good old days. I was out the yard one day, bickin it with No Exit then Boopdaville walked over and asked us both questions. It was more like directed towards me, how long I was put on to the set. He said he asks because that's how he determine, who is who how they carry them selves within this brim gang.

Then turn around and said, I like your mentality I got a book for you to read do you read. I asked him what kind of book, his reply was history literature I read it. The book is called "What They Never Told You In history Class" that book changed my life. Taught me so much that we wasn't taught in school, the more I read the more my mind started elevating. Taught me who was the first president, show me what the first Statue of Liberty looked like. For the record George Washington is not the first president and the Statue of Liberty that we know today is not it. I recommend everybody read and get that book.

From that point on I started looking at things different slowly. They call me over the loudspeaker one day, I head to the receptionist in front building, I was greeted with some papers about gang enhancement. Informing me I had 5 years of it and I couldn't live in the state of New Jersey. My response was how you going to kick me out of the state of New Jersey that's where I'm from and my kids. They response was you can visit but not live for 5 years in the state of New Jersey. I grabbed my copy shook my head and walked out, got back to the population the homies ask me what that was about.

Once I told them what it was they ask me can they do that I'm like it's already done. By this time I'm just waiting for the U.S. Marshals to come and get me. In you wouldn't guess who reappeared this fool Los. I remember him saying he had to do over four years, it was only about 3 year's. When I was told that he was home I knew something wasn't right. Nobody did nothing to him when he checked in PC though, far as being out in the street. I inform everyone that he checked in PC. Mostly everybody that claim they were big homies at that time, was dealing with him for they personal greed. You'll all see how it bit everyone all in they asses and crippled brim as we speak. Big Sha out there in the streets pressing the line hard and guess who else home now. Saleem!

The only person that got their hands on Los, at the county jail was Mush. Next thing you know it was a big Federal sweep, at Newark Airport waiting on the Bounty Hunter Bloods to get off the plane coming from L.A All 3 Bounty Hunter sets Lot Boys, Outlaw and 5Line Bounty Hurter Bloods were all snatched up by the feds. By this time they went out to Watts California, to have a sit-down out in the Nickerson Gardens the birth of Bounty Hunters Bloods with the Ogs. Settle all they differences to bridge the gap become one again. This all happened in 2008 after that the U.S. Marshals come and get me.

THE FEDS WELCOME TO OTISVILLE

US Marshals are waiting for me where the reception area at in Northern State Prison. They take me down to the Federal Building in downtown Newark. I was only there because they had to pick up a few more people that was in federal court. It wasn't clear that I was going to Essex County or Hudson County. By this time Killa E and Blood Money in Essex County Federal tier. They decided to take me to Essex County, when I get their to Essex County it was on to lockdown. They too were popping on the correctional officers, like we were down Northern State Prison.

Reason being when the police killed unarmed Sean Bell out in Queens New York, the day before his wedding with 50 shots. Regardless what we did being a blood, during my times it really meant something. Anywhere we catch a correctional officer down Northern State they got popped on. The greatest part they were all rookies. Right after the verdict we got it Bracken, a solid revolution. Now at Essex County they locked in for the same reason and also Beven gang and Tech gang giving Neighborhood Bloods the business making a lot of them check in PC. The federal tier I got on first where Blood Money, Brim Lock was at. Brim Lock was locked up since "97" for a hot one or two and two attempted murders.

His case wasn't federal though, he was going back to court trying to get some time back. Said his case was looking good, Blood Money .... he started complaining to Killa E like hell no me and B G oh hell nooooo I laughs he like see you can get him off this tier all he want to do is trip. B G wasn't there he was still down Northern State Prison. He were just speaking on B G past, I'm laughing the whole time but at the same time trying to catch my breath like blood I'm not even tripping. Blood Money reply yeah not yet.

I bick it with them fools that night, then next day I was moved to where Killa E was at. By this time it was about three years since we were face-to-face, this when I found out my relative Kaka was on the federal tiers. I was asking him how he was holding up, he had lost a little brother not too long ago. My younger relative KD R.I.P.... By this time I inform Killa E about the fool from L.A like how he let everybody know he leaving at the last second but leaving out of the state of New Jersey. That shit didn't sound right, and this when it came out who were messing with this buster Los after he checked in PC.

By this time Killa E talking on the phone with a nobody, blood was a nobody because he did over 20 years in prison claiming he a Og and never did shit for the set on the streets, never cK never pressed no lines never ride for the set or nothing. Silly shit I'm talking about. The homie on the phone complaining how Big Sha and Killa not respecting him, me I found humor the whole time on the situation. Mind you already know what both of them said to the homie by Killa E, I asked anyway laughs. What they say to you homie, his reply they on some bullshit, I'm like nah what they say to you.

They said I never put in no work for the set I just bust out laughing with Killa E. I said how you expect homies to respect you, when nobody don't even know you and you got put on in there (prison) that shit don't count homie, then most importantly nobody don't care about who gave what. It's about respect who pave the way. You just calling people trying to give out orders for your personal gain this not what being a blood is about. After that he went and start crying to Killer Reek. By this time Killa, Big Sha and Maniak Maine pressing line hard. I was at Essex County for about like a month or two, me and Killa E just reminiscing.

I said X Man was still was alive, we would have been 5 2 Hoover Crips. That's what X Man was, anybody paid attention he barely wore red I always knew. Me personally I didn't pursue it because Crips were killing Crips to me that was just non sense. No disrespect. if I have to watch my own what is the point of me being that. That's the crazy part though Bloods kill Bloods out in state of New Jersey more than Crips, where is though Crips kill more Crips out the state of California more than they do bloods. Far as in the gang banging world. It was beyond a disgrace bloods killing bloods, bloods were going at each other so much and getting caught up in gang sweeps it's the very reason that Crips got bigger in Jersey.

It's almost about that time for me to leave at this County, a correctional officer said some slick shit to the homie next door to us. Killa E got on his ass, I was already on the side of the correctional officer he pleaded to Killa E. Few days later I was on my way, I was sent to MDC Brooklyn a holding facility for federal inmates. Let me tell you that whole building was vicious, I'm at the receptionist desk. One of the correctional officer read my file. They immediately asked do I no B G, I reply why you ask. On West Side Brims every correctional officer down there stop were they doing and listen what I had to say.

In what if I do, they said we are not putting you two together New York Bloods are not used to how Jersey Bloods carry that gang shit. New Jersey bloods on a whole another level, they said whoever he ran into that wasn't a west side brim set was getting popped or he was making them become Fruit Town Brim.

They said B G been in and out of lockup since being there. Right before they send me upstairs to the housing unit, they said we already knew who you were from your file. They would deny if they weren't deep around they homies, you and B G haven't each one of you by yourself it's like you're very proud.

My reply was, if you're not proud then what is the point. It's about 101 inmates on a federal tier, my bunk is by a mobster. I could sense he just watching me and seeing how I move. 1 day it's like he picking my brain, and I'm going to be honest. It was about how I feel about snitches, my reply instantly were it's not just a snitches it's those that deal with the snitches. They are more dangerous than actually the snitches, they all deserve caskets. From there we started building, I'm sitting here listening to him in my head though I'm like damn he just did 25 years for that shit. His supposed to be Mob the Gambino Family were snitching on him he was facing life.

Still haven't a snitch on nobody after doing 25 years, his words exactly was from what I'm a part of you apart of anybody else everybody snitching. And I mean everybody, those that you think won't will. I didn't reply regardless if, I feel the same way or not the more you listen the more you catch a gem within the message. 95 people on our tier were snitching or working for the federal government. Every Sunday at MDC Brooklyn, federal government letting inmates out to work undercover. I couldn't believe what I was seeing, letting people out to set up they friends whomever so they can get less time or do no time at all. After they set up whomever, they switch they whole identity and send you to a whole other state or coast.

Days later they shout my name over the loudspeaker Julius Jones it's time to pack up Otisville next stop. It was a nice long ride way up in the mountains not too far from Ray Brook another Federal Prison. When I say we was up in the mountains man we was up in the mountains for real. We left in the a.m. we didn't get there to that night. They have gang unit in the front as they put in my information in a federal system at the desk. I was brought in a office, immediately Federal gang unit started speaking on my profile. Don't come here bringing that wild wild west shit here, we have fake bloods if you start any of that gang banging mess here. You going to be looking at 120 months running consecutive, I'm like I don't want to be here anyway you can send me somewhere further.

120 months is 10 years, me and nice amount other people were sent to different housing units. As we walking the compound though, I'm observing everything this don't look nothing like no damn prison. To me I called it a daycare center it was that sweet, definitely compared to Northern State Prison. Down Northern State Prison, I seen more people leave in a black bag then actually going home. As I get on my housing unit everyone just looking, keep in mind in the federal prison system you meet people from all over the world. So when new people get off the bus each time, people be hoping they know somebody from they city. I don't have a cell mate, I'm getting sent to the dorm the dorm I was sent to held 18 people.

This where I met La Mass from Jersey City and non affiliated, prior to us meeting in the feds I never seen him we knew quite as the same people. La mass told me that Meeda in Jawz we're in other housing units. In the feds every state has what you call the car, Jersey car California car Upstate New York car then it's the five boroughs. Brooklyn, Staten Island, Queens the Bronx and Harlem but with in each borough there cars within each borough, you talk about politics within the gangs the politics within the federal system is ridiculous. I really don't know if Staten Island is a borough, I just know New York being so big and we were in they state yet they were so divided. If they were more together they would have ran that whole place honestly.

I told La mass I'm on Brim time that's when the conversation automatic switch, he asked me were the Double ii Bloods were they really from a West Coast set. I said of course the first West Coast set birth on the East Coast, he said he heard that but he didn't really know I definitely confirmed it though also let him know mostly Jersey are West Coast sets. I met Alif was from Newark and Boobie from Paterson good men, I spoke to them 4 few then I met a person a Nature Boy from New Orleans. Nature Boy was Bounty Hunter Bloods they were supposed to been claiming from where they from Uptown Bounty Hunter Bloods. A little after that I went back in my dorm, some fool from the Bronx came inside my dorm introduce himself. La Mass right their blood like he Nine Trey Gangster something something line started going into codes I don't know. I'm like this West Side Fruit Town Brims 36th Street Gunna, he like oh you a West Coast set once I said that he immediately left out the dorm.

It was a 18th Street Sureno Gang he was in my dorm his name is Spooky,18th Street started in L.A. Traditionally out in L.A our sets war with one another. From the rip blood was bool as hell, said he'd like how I carried myself with the blood from New York. Also added how he can tell who was really out there pressing the line. 1 dorm yet they were 2 size and one bathroom. It was a Texas Syndicate on the other side of the dorm when you first walk in at. Yet I didn't know that because he was sleep, the very next morning though around 5- 6 a.m.

On every housing unit different Surenos 13 gangs and I say different because it's not just MS 13 that are Surenos. There are different Sureno gangs that are 13s, along with 18th Street all started knifing Texas Syndicate gang, which is that gang from Houston Texas. Alarms is sounding off everywhere you go at, when I get to the chow hall you had one MS 13 sitting right on top of Texas Syndicate. Started digging slowly with the fiberglass, the correctional officers begging MS 13 stop he took it even further M S 13 looking right at the correctional officers now he's knifing the Texas Syndicate neck. I know all of this personally because I was just sitting there watching everything that was going down.

I'm like damn this shit isn't no day care center. The MS 13s and 18th Street took orders from the Mexican Mafia La eMe from out South Central L.A they ran all Sureno gangs, to identify one they had what they called the black hand over their heart tatted. Within the Mexican Mafia there are no leaders, same goes for West Coast blood sets there are no leaders don't let nobody tell you different. The Mexican Mafia was just watching everything play out in the chow hall as well, with blasted tattoos and bald heads. Helicopters came and took like five or six people. Right after that they started snatching Surenos left and right. Surprisingly Spooky was still there, a little after that I go to the front for orientation me quite a few other people.

Talk about blood business he said he was outlaw blood, so I'm like oh you OutLaw 20 Bloods in and outs. He automatic looking puzzle so I could tell he didn't know what, I was talking about. I immediately knew he was representing some made-up shit. On West Side Brims I told him in his face that shit fake, next thing you know a non-affiliated from Brooklyn like we got one you Jersey car fools. Better inform your partner they going to drop them slips and get him out of here. Come to find out they drop a whole bunch of slips on A Dogg a Og from L.A, I was told he went to the dude's from New York that's pushing Blood like listen how they move is not how bloods in L.A move let alone how they push blood. Next thing you know they got A Dogg shipped out.

 As I'm leaving I ran into Jawz and Meeda, Jawz was from Gifford n Bergen and Meeda was from Lexington. Meeda took a couple of charges for Run and a few others so he won't get life in the feds. Jawz was locked up for shotgun, from that day forward we bick it everyday. I had received word that Collar Bone was popping all New York that were claiming the 5 point star representing a west coast set, this was down Ray Brook Federal Prison. Not long after that, I met Akbar Pray at first we just had a very few words to say to one another.

We didn't have nothing against one another, it just was I'm not like everyone else dick riding being a groupie. They said he was the biggest drug lord in state of New Jersey, so the federal system say. The federal system is so cold Akbar Pray honestly in prison for nothing, being this was his first time being locked up. He was talking to his celli, his celli was down with The Supreme Team which is in Baisley Park headquarters in South Jamaica, Queens New York. Akbar Pray express to his celli keep in mind he didn't get no time offered no nothing, he hasn't get caught with a lint of nothing don't you know whatever Akbar Pray said that night in his cell to his celli. I do know his cellmate didn't have a wiretap, when it was time for Akbar Pray to go to court his cellmate popped up keep in mind his cellmate is from The Supreme Team.

Mind you he's in documentaries about his life and so on they have him as a stand-up dude yet he a big snitch. That man repeated everything Akbar Pray said on the stand what was said to him and they cell. Without any wiretap drugs anything gave him life with parole, being this was in the 80s he fall under the old law after you do 25 years. You see the parole board once a year, he's done over 25 years and they still deny him a release date. I meet Murder Ra he from Beven Nine Three out Newark, I didn't have nothing really to say people until I got my paperwork.

I wanted mine ASAP you see in the feds that was like a license, most importantly you can tell who was who. Once I have received mines I went into action ASAP started pushing my paperwork to a lot of individuals. One or two things is going to happen either someone going to push their paperwork back to you, they don't have it or better yet they aren't trying to get it. Don't you know in my housing unit, they had a paper print out on bulletin board for everyone can see it.

That you can get up to 60 months if they found out that you was pressing anybody to show their paperwork. By this time Top shelf was locked up with a P89 and Big Sha also got locked up, the feds both of their cases revolve around gang banging. Going into 2009 was a very vicious year for the brims in the streets and in prison, Hollow Tip is Fruit Town Brick Brim 232, Woozy, Poe, Sha Ru the last three names we're all 793(Beven Nine Three) they all from Newark. Jersey Bloods had they on car from New York Bloods, both cars was representing the five yet Jersey Bloods was not fucking with New York Bloods.

Even though they were represent the five from Jersey, they did not move like New York bloods let alone as if they wasn't pushing that five. New York Bloods were locking the 5 point star with Latin King's they have a alliance with one another. In Jersey its no such thing between any Blood set's and Latin King's. For one theirs so many West Coast sets in the state of New Jersey far as bloods, East Coast sets is going to take a lot from us how we move besides they had experience just like us in wars.

Not only going at West Coast Blood sets, at each other sets and they were definitely cK too. Now Hollow Tip on the compound with me we are the only two that's west side which is perfect. It just show more our strength and we stood out more. New York bloods were deep doesn't matter this Jersey, the second I got there I was already the talk of the compound. Letting them know they fake ass sets, taking our names and making it their own. Bounty Hunters for one, Pirus also saying they bang the five, they have over 30 something stone sets, over nine Brim sets and over 30 something Miller Gangster sets.

I wasn't piecing nobody wasn't greeting nobody or nothing that shit is fake. I was mad as hell every day I was in the feds, I wanted to give it to every last one of them for false flagging. Continuing to misguide mislead, every last one of them is already like two or three sets already I was receiving so much information. They have no Pride about being a blood, just set hopping like this a gimmick and always want to dress all cute. All the sets that was there started they blood set with Nybba. I honestly don't know what it means, I just know it's all wrong.

Me in Hollow Tip bick it we were amazed how all they talk about is what they called lineups and status. Non affiliates from New York they always say they don't gang bang in New York. In a lot of them that were there wasn't even claiming they when they was in other spots further away. Countless from the East Coast don't be claiming they blood until they get around a bunch of people from they state or city or they in they state. As we bick it we talking about the fool from L.A and how out of no where he just left the state of New Jersey.

Nobody heard from him he not responding to nobody letters, moving very suspect. Come to find out the feds snatched him and he knew this whole time they were coming. Not only that things started heating up between the Fruit Town Brick City Brims vs Pirus , 103rd Grape Street Gangster Crips vs 5 Deuce Hoover Crips out Newark and Fruit Town Brims 36th St vs Neighborhood 20 Bloods. A lot of deaths behind Brims vs Pirus who I knew personally that was killed in that war Bishop and Babe B G they both were down Yardville with me. One day in Broad day out in Newark the Grape streets in 5 Deuce Hoover was going back and forth sprained each other sets up with AK-47.

The brims and the doves a lot of homies were dropping, after the homie Rattz was killed shot back of the head then it was Jalil D my little relative. He was killed in broad daylight, they caught him when he had a baby in his arms and told them if they don't kill him he's going to kill every last one of them. His 187 is what started the war from what I was told. After my young relative death the doves started dropping left and right. Back out Newark the Pirus try to spray up a brim homie wake and funeral. By this time over the phone Hollow Tip would bick it with E Trillz he was home from Northern State Prison.

Saying you got to keep a gun on you at all times, that's when we started reminiscing about when we was out there we had to. The Brims out Newark vs Duke Boys that war started behind Hollow Tip relative. He's the one that put on Doo Doo the first Brim that was killed in the state of New Jersey, they shot him from under his chin in the bullet came out the top of his head. He also mentioned when he was frontline on Tech Gang(Duke Boys) 2 of them snitched on his case. As for me I always kept 1 in the chamber I never had to cock back and most importantly my murder weapon was always a revolver, automatic was just a backup.

Half of the time I kept two on me at all times, depending what day how I felt that day what I use. Any everywhere I went I kept mines on me, even when we wasn't warring this shit isn't for play. My mama live directly across from the corner store, I had to have it on me I didn't feel safe without it. When you out their, there's no time to cock back that's how you end up getting killed. Word was sent to us that Killa E and B G were tied into the fool from L.A and a host of other brims that were already in prison.

Then something else happen in the streets, that snitch ass fool Los. He was going around setting people up, let them use this car not just any car. The car had wire taps hidden camcorders, he had even camcorders in his hats as well and his chain working for the feds. He set up a lot of Brim homies, as well a lot of Latin King from out the heights. They all were being around the rapper Akon, the Latin Kings they all grew up together. Los was able to set up the Latin Kings because his brother was the manager that started Akon career.

When he was killed the rappers Fat Joe in Noreaga was there as well Capone. I remember seeing Akon coming to visit the Latin Kings in the county jail. Weeks Later the Nortenos gang got their, once they came on a compound they started popping off on the Sureno gangs. Nortenos gangs flag the color red and the Surenos flag the color blue, the Nortenos mess with blacks. The Surenos be on some racist shit, it's always Black vs Brown the state of California. I also used to be bick it a lot with a Rollin 40 Crip from South Central L.A name were Cisco he too he too use to get irritated. Said he had a sister from L.A 109 Denver Lanes Bloods I bick it with my rivals more then anything.

Back in the dorm Spooky was my spades partner, we was literally beating everybody in spades.

Us Fruit Town and Brick City Brims make the headlines as the most dangerous gangs on the east coast me in Hollow Tip we knew this thing of ours was completely over. Too many homies was making up stories and moving funny. You see you know what hurts us on east coast as bloods. It's more power within the prison system that control the streets. I always say that is the stupidest thing. In for decade's nobody still doesn't see it, that's our downfall as a whole. All because of greed pride and jealousy from one another, competition who's trying to outdo the next then trying to blame the next person for telling.

The sad part the homies that get put on in jail never seen a Brim block yet catching a federal case behind the set that they never did nothing for on the streets. I haven't called the streets in a while, I always will write you before I call anyone. And when I finally do I get hit with the hardest blow while being in prison. I call my youngest daughter mother, she just like call your mother oh my God call your mother. Your mama said you was going to call me and I'll be the one to tell you, someone killed Tai Quwan. I just took the phone off my ear, like I couldn't believe or understand what she just told me. Looked at the phone and put my ear back on the phone like what you just say to me.

My youngest daughter mama, I'm so sorry they killed Tai Quwan I couldn't even talk no more. I just hung up the phone real slowly and kept my hand on the phone. In slowly looked at everyone that wanted to use the phone next, I wanted anybody to say anything slick they had next they want to use the phone can you get off the phone. That night someone definitely would have died maybe two or three, come find out he pass over a month ago. My mama didn't want nobody to tell me, just got out of lockup for trying to pop correctional officer for allowing the inmate to touch in pass the mail out and saying something racist.

I just stayed away from people for a while, from the information that I have received about my brother which I also talked about in "Invincible Tears Vol 1" he didn't have nobody he could trust to have his back and a lot of things just wasn't adding up to me. By this time Brim Lock was killed outside I was told behind a woman that he disrespected, I'm like damn blood really gave that time back. He still had a lot of time to do, for him to come home to just get killed like damn sorry to say I would have rather him being in prison that way he still would be alive. By this time, I remember the homie that was on the phone complaining to Killa E being disrespected by Big Sha and Killa he was set up by Los same person I told him that check in PC.

He was released from prison, the feds let him have less than 24 hours out on the street before they came and snatched his ass they had him on a wiretap about lining somebody up to get killed and how is that because he wanted Los to do it. Remember Saleem he lined him up to got him locked up in the feds conspiracy to commit murder something like that. He even had Jalil D and Rattz on wiretaps talking about how they was giving people headshots. Los was even trying to lineup Albee Al with the feds, like he was really working for the feds.

I'm like man this shit is over, a lot of homies is dying I'm in my feelings because I felt it should have been double the count fools dying behind one homie getting killed. There's no such thing is eye for eye in gang bangin. You take one of mines we take two or three of yours, it's called one up. If you really on that type of time, you hit your rival set 3 minutes later you bust a cK in hit that shit again, then bust another cK 6 minutes later hit that shit again then we going wait 4 hours clear that shit again it's called a curfew.

That's the type of shit I was on when I was home. By this time Nortenos were very deep at Otisville, Nortenos may refer to Northern California as Norte Califia's. Their biggest rivals are the Surenos from Southern

California, Norte "NXIV" or "N14" so when you say 13 they be like killer laughs. It was also Fresno Bulldogs there which they use F 14. Months down the line I was just observing all the news articles I had constantly I was tired of seeing homies dying and being in prison. I took this business management class, the class was about what you wanted to do in life.

Mines came out to always giving back, it made perfect sense I say that because I used to watch my mama sit at the TV and watch Feed the Children so many homeless kids walking around barefoot and butt naked poor you could really see they bones. They were just starving in Africa that always played in my mind as a child, I had so many questions for my mama but she couldn't answer them.

Even when she didn't have no money, she still sent them $30 a month Feed the Children, so once I got older I will pick randomly 3 different children a month and send $100. I did it for a few years right before I was rearrested of course I couldn't do it no more. Nobody ever knew that I did that, it wasn't about recognition it was something I felt I just needed to do. Anytime I went anywhere to go shopping, I found someone less fortune bought them something to eat and gave them a couple of dollars.

I remember me and my sister Erica will go out shopping and her friends will be with us they catch me buying less unfortunate man some food tell my sister like look what your brother doing, Erica reply will be he always do that. Started talking to La mass about my plans, I wanted to give back and start my own program and redirecting the youth. La mass is actually the first person I ever spoke to about this, from the second I mention it he never once doubted me. From that point forward I just started keeping myself in the dorm, working on my plans and goals when I get out of prison.

Yet to transition from my negativity mindset, to a positive mindset was very challenging. In the beginning I use to battle with myself, all these different voices in my head saying how I turned my back on my set, I don't care about the homies no more if you go a straighten arrow. Nobody's going to respect you no more, I mean I'm really in tears thinking about this shit, I would continuously throw my notepad and everything writing on the floor. Like fuck this shit blood, my homies in the set need me. Then something much greater and powerful hit me, you in here keep worrying about your homies and set.

How many times they came and seen you in wrote you? How many times they checked on your mama? How many times they checked on your daughters? When one of your daughters mother, needed a place to live and bouncing from place to place, where were your homies set at then? You locked up behind, did they bail you out, give you lawyer money? Didn't you do all of that on your own, did they even offer you anything? Then you'll don't owe nobody shit, the only people that you owe is your kids in most importantly your damn self. 2-3 tears drop from the left side of my eye, I was once told anytime the tears drop from the left side of the eye first it means that's pain.

I wanted to give my daughters something to be proud of instead of a image and reputation. My mama brought up my youngest daughter and my middle daughter to see me, she said they need to see you the girls keep asking for you. I didn't want my daughters to see me like this, they were older so they can understand more that they father locked up like some caged animal. When I stepped out to the visitor floor they lit up the whole visiting room, they smiles and they were just pointing at me.

You know what my mama was so right, I just kept saying in my head at that visit. I really have to get my shit together, talk to my mama face-to-face about my plans she was so excited because it's something that she always wanted me to do back in 2002. In what I mean by that, I have received the letter 2002 summer from Integrity Halfway House program and downtown Newark by City Hall. They wanted me to come and speak to kids and get paid while doing it.

All I wanted to do was slang an gang bang though, I told my mama proud fully I found my calling and started really educated myself about literature. From literature to civil rights to spirituality, really have something to talk about other than this the streets gangs. Then one day, I went to the legendary Black Panther born Clark Edward change his slave name too Sundiata Acoli codefendant to Assata Shakur. Which is Tupac Shakur auntie which killed the state troopers on Trenton New Jersey highway, even though they case was State they pushed it towards the feds.

Making it impossible for him to get released to this day. A long side though, I also went to Akbar Pray. So, I started walking the yard with these two great men everyday. Then one day Akbar Pray showed me, he helped Mary J Blige and Ludacris with they nonprofit organizations along with a host of other people he done help yet your federal government giving him a hard time to come home though. Later that day a few Latin King's from Chicago came on the compound. When Chicago Latin Kings found out New York Latin Kings let the Bloods in New York claim "Peoples Nation". The Chicago Latin Kings started popping the New York Latin Kings and different Federal Prison.

Anyway back to my story, he was so surprised all the material that I have written out. So Akbar Pray he asked me did you write all this out yourself, my reply was yes I had my sister Riri was always ordering me books when I asked. And this one book in particular we're about grants and how you format sessions proposals etc. So what I did was think back to how me and kids my age always, which elders did with us. Sundiata Acoli have told me I needed to read this book called The Assassination Of Fred Hampton. That book was beyond powerful, then I have my sister buy this book called 1001 Things Everyone Should Know About African-American History. Show you all the inventors which were black men and women, everything in North America was created by us. In this particular book it show you date names and how White America took over.

Out in the streets in Jersey City though, word was 5 Deuce Hoover Crips was going around to different blood sets saying they had no problems with they sets. Yet Sex Money Murder they had to go, the 5 Deuce Hoover Crips started sniping Sex Money Murder, and I mean back to back to back to back to back. I remember reading news article, some Sex Money Murder rode alongside some 5 Deuce Hoover Crips just chilling all in the car and air that shit out. I'm like damn they just caught them slipping like that. Months later Sha Ru from Beven gang snapped on some New York Bloods, Swift from Sex Money Murder also from out Newark. He were trying to keep it peaceful because along with Poe Woozy they were ready to trip.

I believe somebody from New York that just came down, try to question them who gave them permission to start Beven as they should they said nobody. Don't get it twisted they may be riding that 5 out in Jersey they two was really gang bangin as well. So they reply was who gave permission to start any of that shit in New York it's all lies. I was fucking with Poe, Sha Ru, Woozy in them if they were going to pop I was popping to, a lot of them were in the gym. As for me I was speaking to somebody from Boston and as we talking.

Other people from Boston was doing something, yet saying something to the person I was speaking to. They all supposed to be Rollin 40s Crips and 5 9 East Coast Crips, I took it as disrespect like they trying to be funny or something. So, I stopped at his mid conversation walk straight to them like blood any of you have a problem or something. I'm by myself we can get it Bracken, like whatever you all have to say to him say that shit around him homie this is Brim Gang and I mean anybody that was at Otisville Meeda, Jawz, Wise, Poe, Swift, Woozy and Murder Ra to non affiliated I didn't give a fuck no I was pressing the line.

When it came to this Brimin you wasn't fucking with it straight up. They talking about no disrespect man I just walked away, I was saying in my head they would have been on my list to get on the streets. Time goes on I continue rebuilding with Akbar Pray, also letting Hollow Tip know my mentality, he knocked out some fool on his housing unit yet he wouldn't tell me though. One night me and La mass up in the dorm, I'm telling him more about my plans and program that's when he took it even further. La mass like Gunna going to be speaking at High Schools Colleges events like I could see it now.

Truthfully in my head I couldn't see it at that time but he seen it. Later down the line, I definitely started seeing it myself La mass was definitely my motivation and gave me hella inspiration. One day we deep as hell, we all at where we shoot pool at it's a long line where you can sit at. Usually the benches for sit down and wait for your turn to shoot a game of pool, yet fools was taken turn for something else there's a movie room. In that movie room there are multiple chairs and TVs with long tables.

Longs you have some headphones you could pick out pretty much any movie and music watch or listen to. A young person from D.C. was going around collecting books of stamps from a bunch of men and that line they was waiting to get their dick suck in the movie room. By different individuals that were from D.C. I mean these young dudes were young giving out head for books of stamps at a time. Stamps, I'm speaking of stamps that you used to put on an envelope. Their names were Tiny, Toya and Pinky, the movie room used to be so crowded dudes would bring their coats to shield what they were doing in there (getting head).

One day somebody from Brooklyn New York ask me a serious question, what he representing does it have anything to do with what I'm representing. I'm like no, I said oh boy telling you Bounty Hunter started at Hunter's Point that's in the Bronx. The home of Nickerson Gardens which is in Watts California is the birth of all Bounty Hunter Bloods homie. There's no such thing as no Godfather, you see how after you piece put your hand over your heart that's La eMe Mexican Mafia gang homie, everything that fool has you doing is wrong don't have nothing to do with being a blood homie.

Speaking in codes wearing religious bees, oaths pledges none of that don't exist. It is the reason why I don't shake nor speak to none of them. They all no this yet they refuse to fix it, can't say you love something you don't even have no understanding what you apart of. No West Coast blood sets ride the five homie, only in the Jays that have ties to the five that's it that's all everyone on this compound lying it's the reason why everyone stay away from me because I exposed them....

When a Lot Boys Bounty Hunter Blood from Asbury New Jersey got there, he definitely set the record straight and told them none of them in they face are Bounty Hunter Bloods. They don't even say what hood they are they just say the set. It's impossible for anybody in New York to just say they are Bounty Hunter Bloods. The only way you can say you are just Bounty Hunter Bloods, if you was there from the beginning that's it that's all. Just like any other set after the set starts to become branch offs and hoods, it's beyond sad that nobody takes the time to really find out what they become apart of yet everybody love being a blood though.

Akbar Pray tells me he's pushing for us to get certified certificate consultant, I should join him. So I did, Semaj my Og from Stegman n Ocean he was their proud of me, that particular day I was speaking to some High School freshman. After that was over the so-called professionals that had the black and white, pacifically said if we allowed them to get certified in this prison. We will lose our careers in the streets, yet the system believe in so much a second chances. We never got a chance to get certified.

The very next day something exclusive happen, this person from Jamaica Queens. He had 27 years to do he never missed a visit his best friend which was the godfather of his daughter. He been coming to see him 2 years straight faithfully, gave her a big sweet 16 party, senior graduation party and most of all pay for college tuition. For the love of his homie he thought had the same love for him. Come to find out the person from Jamaica Queens, was wearing a federal wire the whole time got him 30 to life and he was released from the feds. Cold game....

They knew each other their whole lives and he did him like that, doesn't matter how long you knew a person what you went through with that person. A snake is just a snake. When that came out that he was wearing a federal wire, a lot of other people started moving very suspicious. On every housing unit there's a phone at the end of the hall, that's directly connected to the prosecutor's office. Just in case anybody find out any new information on somebody to get you another Federal indictment. I really appreciate myself that I was never the type to always want to brag and boost what the hell I was doing to prove a point.

I used to always be building with this god body five percenter, mind you he had life for countless people even his own family members snitching on him. Be the main one always talk about snitches, going try to make an excuse why he deal with this particular snitch. Told blood stay away from me man, like how you dealing with a snitch when you in here for snitches giving you life. Told him in his face anybody that deal with a snitch is a snitch they damn self. Word was going around that people from Jersey was really sticking they chest out about War Stories in extra shit. I've have yet to seen fools paperwork though, so I told Meeda, Jawz, Kooda, La Mass and Hollow Tip.

That I'm pressing the issue I'm tired of everybody mouth, Woozy and them had theirs though it was these non-affiliated. slowly but surely a lot of things started coming out how so many was making excuses that they've been there three or four years already. I don't care about none of that shit show that shit or stay away from me, matter of fact none of you fools isn't brim anyway. People cards started getting pulled, Akbar

Pray pull me to the side, like Gunna just leave it alone they scared to show it just let them be.

From that point forward I have done nothing with Jersey as a whole. Individuals I dealt with, everyone needs to understand to over stand every Federal Prison 95% of the people that's at the prison are snitches. 95% of the federal system 60% of them are snitches and 35% of them are going out there to work as federal informant, keeping in mind most people that come from the feds don't ever speak of it let alone show they paperwork. You ever want to see anybody paperwork, get the U S Marshal number once you get there U S Marshal number now you can find out the plea agreement you want to see docket sheet you want to see the sentencing minutes in a trial transcripts nothing else matters.

Never want to see I repeat never want to see a presentence report I know I said that before it's very important because it's not paperwork. This what everybody favorite rapper and big homie showing. About two three months later Otisville started kicking everybody out that was in a gang from the state of California and the state of New Jersey talking about we too aggressive they don't want us their.

Oh by the way, I was shooting the fade I was getting the best of blood until he grabbed my locks. From that point on blood could have did me dirty honestly because he grabbed my locks yeah he didn't even do nothing. As a man I take it as a loss, the following morning he didn't feel comfortable being on the same unit as me and move to another housing unit. Then I was told to pack up I'm getting transferred. I didn't even know where I was going at but I knew that was the last stop.

Finally Stop Fort Dix Federal Prison

It's 5 a.m. in I'm getting ready to leave Otisville Federal Prison, the U S Marshals take us to MDC Brooklyn as a quick stop to pick up more inmates. We switch buses I didn't find out I was actually going to Fort Dix Federal Prison until we pull up to the spot. Now this place I tell you look like a whole circus, there were no type of rules regulations no nothing. The biggest Federal Prison it holds 5,000 inmates, Eastside and Westside which holds 2,500 inmates on each side....

When you first get to Fort Dix you automatic on the west side, on the west side has a building where they decide if they going to keep you on the Westside population or take you to the east side population. I met a Piru homie from East Orange I forget his name I like how he was bumming though, he was exactly speaking the same language I was speaking. By the way he was from 464 Insane Mob Piru, he was saying he was just over all the Piru Brims and Bloods dumb shit. Like when was the last time I have heard any homies killing any Crips, all I could do is shake my head. He also added you can't even just pull up to any blood hoods anymore.

The Mob Piru homie like what is the point, he apologized for reminiscing and expresses himself. He said it just hard to find like-minded homies and I felt the need to get it off my chest my reply is I couldn't agree with you more homie that's why I just let you talk. It is when I ran into Ace from Wegman n Jackson my other Og he was expressing how hurt he was when he heard of Tai Quwan passing. I just looked away for a few minutes, then lock eyes with him. If I was home and anybody that were related to whomever had killed Tai Quwan first I would have killed the person who did it. Then I would have went to the person funeral, I done killed to see if he had a brother grieving over him and kill him as well.

B G

I think about Tai Quwan literally everyday I was on the west side for a few days probably about a week, right before I'm headed to the east side couple of East Side Bloods from New York came to me saying they were some other type of brims said we need to stick together. My reply if you're not going by the original protocol the rules and regulations there's nothing for us to discuss. It's impossible for any one of you to tell me you love something that you have no understanding about, the following morning I packed up and headed to the east side.

This when I get a full understanding how things were in Fort Dix, Fort Dix looked like little bitty in Newark. I met a homie name Woochie from Sacramento California he from Meadowview Blood 23rd Block, Skeem from Baltimore he is Tree Top Piru, Twenty is 5 Line Bounty Hunter Bloods from Kentucky in the homie Kock Back from Baltimore he is 4 Line Bounty Hunter Bloods. At this particular building, I was there temporarily I introduce myself Fruit Town Brims 36th Street Gunna from Jersey.

They were telling me all type of things that were going on the eastside. For starters a Fruit Town Brim homie he wasn't even claiming brim, he was on Muslim time from Camden New Jersey. The homie Woochie express to me how he felt, like how blood even blood but he not claiming it. Then he let some Eastside fools discipline a Fruit Town Brim homie an embarrassment I was tight inside I'm not going lie. It was about some homeboy from South Jersey on some same sex allegations.

The homie Twenty and me got real tight, I built with the homies everyday but our conversations be deeper then just gang ties. Talking about our kids our mother's and just elevating in life. I would share my plans with him about me working with the youth, in life you can't share your plans with everyone most people be in competition with you or just jealous and envy of you. Few days later I was moved down to another unit, and for the life of me I forget all the homies names that were from Jersey.

It was a homie from Trenton he was G-Shine he had the car for them I guess the blood car. Keep in mind no West Side homies ever mention no car to me, regardless that car don't matter to me I'm Brim. We always move on our own accord. G-Shine homie breakdown what was taking place with the homie from South Jersey. In that the homie from Camden allow the East Side homies to DP brim homie. By this time I was meeting all types of gangs from Chicago, Chicago was deep as hell down there.

You had Almighty Vice Lord Nation, Black Disciples, Almighty Black P Stone Nation, Spanish Cobras, Four Corner Hustlers, Mickey Cobras, Gangster Disciples, Maniac Latin Disciples and the Blackstone Ranger. The Gangster Disciples and Maniac Latin Disciples I really started bickin it with first. The Gangster Disciples in the Black Disciples we're saying yeah we have a real Brim down here now, it were about three different sets of from New York saying they Brim I never heard of in my life. Something called Low Rida Brims, Murder 1 Brims & Mac Baller Brims, I'm like where the hell they come up with this mess.

I heard so many different stories, I don't know where to start. They all wanted me to put them on, I'm like blood you all grown men and I don't put anybody on in prison let alone no one man make a decision put anybody on. I'm like I don't even know none of you let alone you all don't know me. A reputation don't mean nothing it can always be bought. In again getting put on in prison not respected in my book, I don't know how much time you all have left but I advise you all to go out to L.A and find out the truth. I'm definitely going out there once up get settled, I would have been out there already if I would have never got re arrested this what I tell them.

By this time it's a lot of snitching going on within Fruit Town in Brick City Brims. In this coming from those that never been brim blood or nothing on the streets, to me that was just ridiculous getting caught in a conspiracy about being blood. I remember being back at Northern State Prison it was this particular evening and everybody's on the same line on the phone. I can honestly say, I knew something was going to go down. Why I said that because that's the same way the feds got Sex Money Murder out in Jersey City.

Fort Dix

Everyone connected to one line all it takes for that one person to be working then it becomes a domino effect. In that 's what happened now homies are connected to Baltimore we didn't even know it was Fruit Town Brims in Baltimore. They weren't just Fruit Town Brims though, they were Fruit Town Southside Brims. I remember being asked do I want to use the phone that same night everybody from different prisons even on the streets were on the phone that night. I'm like know I'm not getting on with nobody I haven't met face to face let alone even no I'm bool homie. It was even a woman from Jersey City that were even picked up by the feds, turn around was release and now all of something she haven't been seen since.

I told his silly ass that she is snitching, the feds when they got you they got you they not letting you go unless you working. How you get picked up by the feds and they let you go the next day. Days later I met a homie name D from L.A he was actually Fruit Town Brims, he had a son or two by the snitch from L.A one of his sisters either Tina or Nene. I believe he was originally from Belize he didn't deal with nobody as well not even a conversation with the homie from Sacramento. The only person he would bick it with were me, also let me tell you all this.

Again Fort Dix is the biggest Federal Prison, 5,000 inmates out of five thousand inmates 3,700 inmates were child molesters and rapists. Theirs nothing but dorms at Fort Dix Prison, 6 child molesters were in my dorm. I made they life a living hell, I was pissing on they sheets and blankets, commissary were getting taken. Every time a new homie came on a compound a child molesters were paying for the cosmetics in food. A lot of child molesters have restraining orders on their own kids. A lot of so call real niggas we're supporting child molesters, and what I mean by supporting child molesters these real niggas.

When you working in the kitchen you get ODR food, you get fresh fruits onions tomatoes lettuce you name it even plates of food. The child molesters ran the kitchen, so the child molesters were selling these things on the compound and everyone were buying their food, I'm not buying nothing I'm taking it. They even ran what movies were being played on movie night, they love picking out kids movies. One day on the west side a non affiliated was pressing his daughter mother about not receiving his pictures of his daughter birthday party. She kept telling him that she sent them, so one morning someone else walked past a child molester room he had his locker door wide open. That person seen the non-affiliated daughter pictures hanging inside the child molester locker. The non-affiliated stuck a broomstick inside the child molester ass and he was being raped by the broomstick.

Weeks later the homie Maniak Maine arrives, the homie from Camden brings him to me. So much going on during that time, I didn't know who was who back home. When I first seen him I was happy but I asked him you still Brim right his response was like hell yeah, wess Brimin my response is brim gang or don't bang....

As we catching up in bick it he tells me the fool Los, lined his ass up prior to him getting arrested by the feds. He said Los kept pressing him to deal with a certain individual, that's what made him stop dealing with Los. The whole time I just shook my head, like if everybody would have just listened from the door the average person wouldn't of had a federal case in the first place. Not long after Maniak Maine came down, the homie Rocky he's from Kansas City. He bang where he's from, Kansas City Bix Deuce Brim, he never knew about bloods on the East Coast at all.

We instantly became tight, we were on the same housing unit I received a letter from Juelz saying I'm almost at the finish line. Kock Back in Twenty were shipped out before Rocky in Maniak Maine got there. You had a homie I believe from Long Island, let me tell you about this weird shit. He's lucky I forget his name, he tells me he's a Westside Brim and how he started his own hood. He had his own brother go out to the turf out L.A in met with Sugar Bear and other's, I never got the others names.

To get his own set, twisted part his brother wasn't even blood he was an non affiliated, it doesn't even matter though he wasn't even Brim in first place. Little did I know when it came to the turf it was so much dumb shit going on it was past ridiculous. Not only after he did that for his brother he decides to get put on to 104 Crenshaw Mafia Bloods. At first I really thought he was joking, like this can't be real this what it came down to. I knew right there that he had to be paying at that time it was called Red Line Mafia Bix Deuce Harvard Park Brim.

How I know all of this, it was a homie named Bully he aces 6 1 Harvard Park Brim he had Sugar Bear on a loudspeaker from a cell phone. I'm telling the homies they thought I was joking too, a fool from St Louis another person that I would bick it with everyday he was St. Louis Rollin 60 Crips, they were the first set in St Louis back in the late 70s very early 80s. His name was Eye used to be me Eye and Rocky in the back watching movies speaking on our plans when we get out. By this time I show Rocky and Maniak Maine how to get their paperwork. In the feds you only have 30 days to show your paperwork.

I say about a good 4 or 5 months later, some wild shit hit my ears. The homie from Long Island, the so called have his own set. Allow a person from North Carolina tell him to suck his dick, he didn't do shit. Me Maniak Maine and Rocky sitting at the chow hall, Maniak expresses himself to me. I tell Maniak Maine tell that fool when he pull up. I'm not going to hold you, I thought Maniak Maine was going to pop him.

The fool from Long Island like he had a talk with oh boy, we all three like a talk you were supposed to knife his ass. Some other fool he was from the Bronx, said he had his own set he was put onto Leuders Park Pirus. I'm saying in my head another person just trying to look cute, in the turf just giving out like government cheese. Something devastated family happen again, it finally comes out that Vincent Young is a cold snitch. Snitched on correctional officers, told the Feds who he put on as guards, who is bringing in the cell phones weed liquor.

He snitch so much it's 100 sheets of paper I only seen 10. Within that 10 he named everybody from up north New Jersey. He snitch on the homies from Baltimore. His plea was life in the feds he only got 14 years and I believe 7 months. He knew the feds were coming this whole time, he try to literally throw everything on Killa Reek. He had got a homie named Red Rum from Baltimore life in prison. It's who Vincent put on started Fruit Town Southside Brims. They all got swept in a big case as well, Blood literally blame everybody else but himself. Once I told the homie D from L.A about his so-called brother-in-law being a snitch.

Blood fell back from me I believe he fell back he didn't know what to say once I told him Vincent's snitched on the whole state of New Jersey. By this time I get word about No Exit, homies trying to trip on blood. When he get out of lockup, he started a knifing homies left and right that try to trip on him. By this time Killa E take 30 years, B G took 35 years they both were facing the death penalty and life twice behind this Brimin.

Maniak Maine headed to the halfway house then I was next. My father reappear while I was down in Northern State Prison, I must say that it was very weird sitting at that visiting room with him. He offer for me to start my life over as well I couldn't go back to Jersey anyway I was kicked out of living in the state of New Jersey. So I agree opportunity to start all over, right before my release the feds stopped at my father house.

Told my father they didn't want me to live in the state of Virginia, so they brought some papers for him to sign stating that he agree he doesn't want me live in the state of Virginia neither. When he refused they told him if I brought any wild wild west gang banging to they state. They would definitely going to finish me in the feds left my father doorstep. The next week I was called early next morning to pack up to get released from prison....

Da Journey Is Over Welcome Home

As I wait for the front gates to open up. I lift my head up to the sky as the gates opening up I take a deep breath of fresh air. From that moment I realized the very simplest thing we take for granted seeing pigeons cats and dogs squirrels run around. I say this there were a lot of people supposed to get out before me or with me. Hot one cases were popping up on them right before they release date. I have a nice little ride to catch down south. At first trying to figure out how to use this card, I had money on there from my prison account I was a little frustrated I didn't know how to use it or even no how to get the money off the card.

We stopped at a Delaware station I believe I was on the Greyhound. As I'm online I feel all the attention on me. People were saying they could tell I did a lot of time and once again I found myself not knowing what to do with this card. Elderly woman walk me through the steps how to order food off my card, I feel someone else staring at me. As I look at the young lady I tell her something crawling on her eye, come to find out it was her eyelash.

Didn't mean to embarrass her I was fresh out of prison I didn't know that was the style to me it was tacky the drawing eyebrows the big flipper eyelashes countless woman getting but interjections fixing they nose. It was very limited run into a black woman that really value herself. And what I mean by that she appreciated what she was born and created with. On my way to Virginia I was happy but I wasn't excited. At the same time while I was headed to the federal halfway house.

My mama her siblings were burying they youngest sister she passed from stage 4 cancer. She knew for nearly a decade and never told nobody, by time her best friend told the family it was too late. I was told this was the first time my mama really smiled, it wasn't really force she was really very happy. Finally one of her sons are home. My aunt Doris wish that passed from cancer.

She was their that night when I left a fool body twisted, I knew she was down because she never said nothing about it. To me most importantly to our family, just that same night that it happened she scream my name got me in the car drop me off home. Before getting out the car though, just kept saying you one of the strong nephews that we have left in this family and I love you.

Months before getting released from prison, I had talks with my mama identical twin Jeanette, Aunt Martha Aunt Doris. They all knew I had anger so much anger towards a family, they all just wanted me to start off with a new life. I appreciated it that conversation with my aunt Doris. I remember before getting off the phone, I told her. I took care of that situation that happened behind one of her nieces her reply was I know. By this time my relative Sosa done pass away as well.

That's all I knew was death. About 45 minutes before I get to the halfway house, I asked can I use someone's phone. I called Sam so he can meet me there, and bring the things I needed for the halfway house. Juelz bought me a lot of socks boxes and tank tops. Keep in mind Juelz stay out in ATL, when he flew out to Jersey he contacted my mama and bought the things in dropped it off to her. He would I considered a real friend, my whole prison term all he did was encourage me to be a better man.

A week after I got rearrested until a week before getting released from prison. He was their didn't miss a beat, the only other person I heard from time to time throughout the years was my brother Naim. It felt weird being back on the outside but I was still in the halfway house though. I was talking to Julissa and Zy'onna every day while I was in there as well my oldest Princess.

I called each one of them every day before they went to school. Finally federal gang probation officer came to see me, I was patiently waiting. He asked how I was doing, being in the new strange environment. He knew I wasn't from Virginia and I didn't have no family. My reply was great and I'm comfortable wherever I go at. Then got right to it, do you have any plans goals.

So, I had show him a folder that I had from federal prison. Format the name of my program organization the sketches of my business card I drew up. Having different class session for the kids and the young teenagers. Sketching out shirts sweaters and logos. He was very impressed, his reply was shocking though.

He said I was the first and only person that actually had a plan before getting out. In that he know I will not return again, he say you too passionate to give up. He said I'm confident you will be off federal probation very early. That night I was speaking to a young homie he was home Fly Ti he was from Jersey City. The last time I seen blood is the night I got arrested, matter of fact came to the bounty see me once. Right before going to college to play football, I remember a situation happen with a homie sister.

When we get there the young homie Fly Ti call himself getting out the car. I'm like where you think you going there, me and Mr.187. Told blood this isn't for you, you the future stay your ass in that car. I remember his ass bringing a homie from East Orange. Fly Ti tell Mr.187 about the young homie and our reply was you know he got a cK right and before that he got to hang around the hood. We don't know that fool you do, that same night blood was with us though.

We was supposed to test the young homie out, instead me and Mr. 187 hop out laughs.... Those were the days.. I'm speaking to Fly Ti over the phone though, at the halfway house he's excited. Like I'm coming to visit you can you get visit yet. This when everything start turning around, keep in mind we was lied to about everything far as our set. By this time everybody, so divided it was past a disgrace. This one wanted to be bigger than this one. Endless perpetrating those playing the role of being somebody, here it go I knew none of them.

You see back then you didn't need to know everybody but you knew of the person name. We weren't this deep being a brim, a Westside Brim at that it really meant something. I was finding out firsthand how was everywhere on the East Coast now. While in prison I didn't really talk to nobody, I was force on surviving doing my time I didn't cared about the streets. That's how you catch new cases, you don't know who getting picked up recording your conversations or nothing. The objective is to get your time do your time and get out. Not catch a new cases while doing your time.

Back to Fly Ti though, blood start telling me all types of wild shit. In now fool's going out there to L.A. So blood like man this person got to be somebody he

going out there. I said blood it doesn't matter who go out there to L.A have you been known him anybody else out here in these streets for that matter. Most importantly who known him from my generation and before. So let me get this straight everyone basically being a groupie because he went to L.A and met Melly Mel in the homies.

That's wess bracken blood went out there but he isn't nobody and he definitely lying he isn't no big homie. Didn't you say blood was playing football he was all American. In he from North Bergen these fools lying they don't know that fool. Mind you I peep every body motive from the door. I didn't want no parts of nobody, all this fake brim love brim that. Fly Ti tells me this same fool tells him he going to bick it with a homie from out Jersey City. Fly Ti like blood isn't nobody man you need to talk to Gunna.

None of these fools were around. When I spoke to blood I told blood he isn't nobody dead homies. Anybody going to the turf that shit don't mean nothing to me. I put this shit on my back 24/7, nobody out here was doing the shit I was doing before I got re arrested nobody. They didn't know nothing what Brim love and Damu love is. Everyone out here were just in competition with one another trying to prove who go to L.A first and what they was saying to whoever they was speaking to out in West Side South Central L.A .... In again my generation and the generation before me, don't know none of these fools from nowhere.

Name any state any city nowhere, Fly Ti come from Raleigh N.C to Virginia we finally meet. He brought a homie at that time with him from Raleigh N.C I can honestly say he seem bool, from that day forward since me being out of prison. I met about two homies I felt that was brim material. I say that it was just a bunch of put on. This shit was really just a fashion show. I didn't feel no love brim love nowhere, everyone doing thumbs down now. Getting tattoos making shirts for the hood, haven't put no work in behind the set.

He introduced me to a home girl named Menika, she didn't even really know me yet she gave me $150 for my daughters. That touch me in a real way because I honestly didn't feel comfortable seeing my daughter's without having something to give them. I went to go see my federal gang probation officer, ask him can I see my daughters. He said usually you have to wait 90 days before being out of prison. But he knew I just did a lot of time, so he okayed it.

He sternly kept saying if I feel, I'm about to get into any trouble come back to Virginia. I'm very serious Julius they don't want you out in the streets. I'm like they who, gang task force contacted me the second you got out of prison. I'm like damn I haven't been out 3 days yet, he like Jersey don't even want you back in Jersey at all. Once I was approved I can go to Jersey.

First he let me know I had to have a home phone number for him. He needed the address, if I was going anywhere else he needed a home phone number from that address as well. If I get caught without his permission, going to another state that's automatic violation back to prison. Also inform me about the monthly report I had to send, that's right once a month. Every month on the 5th day being stamped by the post office it's about 10 questions yes or no answers.

If that report not sent back on time, that's automatic violation sent back to prison. Took a piss test, now I'm on my way headed to Jersey. This when it finally hits me, my relative Sosa is gone but what hit the hardest my brother Tai Quwan. The last we were face-to-face was the night of my arrest, I remember when he wrote me I still have the letter to this very day. Speaking on how people hating on me, even said it to my youngest daughter mother as well. I just couldn't grasp the concept, me being out of prison he wasn't here to celebrate with me. Two of the main woman of my life, pick me up from the station.

My sister Riri and Twin Twin, I couldn't believe how Twin Twin got so big. I help raised her till, I went to prison and now she's a young lady. She wrote me a lot of times even show me her designs, cause she was into graphic design. Take me to see my mama Maryanne she's excited happy I'm finally out. I was patiently waiting to see my daughter Zy'onna. When I first seen her she was knocked out in the backseat. At first she was very shy and surprises finally see me out of prison. Had a nice time that night tucked her in.

Following day I went to go see Julissa. Before that my mama pick me up, hopped out the car with tears happy with joy that I'm finally out. Now we headed to go see Julissa, when I hopped out my mama bought her a bike. I bent down walking with it, once I popped up Julissa didn't pay attention to the bike.

She ran into my arms I was happy as hell to finally see my kids. Then I stopped by to see my oldest, when she finally realize I was at the door she hugged me so tight I can barely breathe. I was in Jersey for about 11 to 12 days. While I was in Jersey my federal probation hit me. I'm like is everything all right, he asked me if I'm okay I'm like yes why you ask that. Cause I was contacted by the state of New Jersey gang task force. In somebody from Jersey contacted them to let them know, that you was in town.

I'm like I'm not even doing nothing, my family won't let me walk to the corner store. He like Julius promised me be careful. This when I first see Facebook, keep in mind when I was first got locked up. Facebook Instagram Myspace didn't exist. I started deleting a lot of people, my sister Riri made an account for me. It was people on my page I started deleting they were snitches in dealing with snitches themselves.

Next thing you know it somebody contact whomever on Facebook I guess. Said I was still in prison in they deleted my whole account. I'm back out Virginia job hunting, that's when I meet a homie named Dollarz from Asbury New Jersey. Blood was bool he was just around somebody that was perpetrating to be a big homie. Somebody else that got put on in prison, yet never been to a brim set in Newark. In he from Newark. Dollarz was the first person to actually show me all the social media banging that was going on.

It was so many different Harvard Park Brim sets, I just knew fools is paying for these shits. Nobody from any where can tell me any different.

Everyone was like two or three different sets and now all the sudden, is that they have they own Westside brim sets. Everybody respected this shit, like really respecting it, No Kuttz No Smutt....

I don't know no other set where the trees grow tall and the fruits grow strong this all I know. You have Harvard Park Brims this Harvard Park Brims that, none of these fools isn't shit. Same goes for Van Ness Gangster Brims, now everybody on the East Coast want to be West Side Brims all of something. Where everybody was at when the wars was going on, everybody was scared to be a Westside Brim. Let alone Fruit Town Brims and Brick City Brim....

By this time I finally found me a job. Goes out to Richmond Virginia on hood day. Faking everybody got a hundred million flags on with no burners on them. The fool at time he kept worrying about how L.A was doing it. I'm like blood you keep worrying about the turf, when you don't even know how to be a blood. You got put on in prison. At this time I was working minimum wage, $ 8.75 Hour part time as a dishwasher.

Still took the time out, to write send pictures buy stamps, birthday cards Father's Day cards. Nobody out here was doing that at all. By this time I done met young homie named Lace from New Brunswick New Jersey. Another young homie misguided left stranded. I started connecting with the home girls, one of the first home girls I connected with was the home girl Tip. She's from Hackensack New Jersey, then it was Red Pit she from Raleigh North Carolina. Home girls have more heart than these so-called homies and big homies. Wasn't surprising though, the things that they was telling me I'm like all that shit is wrong. Around this point on I'm building with my first relative Trey almost everyday. He was surprised how much I grew mentally, you see I was moving around. I wasn't outside on the block, I was outside though I was interacting with the home girls.

When you see the home girls, they see how you carry yourself you move different you isn't coming at them like everybody else is they going to fuck with you. I wasn't doing what everybody else were doing, kicking each other backs in. Who were dealing with who more, the home girls were asked me. Like I told them I tell anybody we all one we all Brims.

Homies didn't have the home girls back like they were supposed to though. I was getting on everybody asses.

That's the least everybody could do they weren't doing nothing else. Down the line I met a home girl name Killa Girl and home girl Ashanti they both were from Newark. I must say though they both check who I was before actually having a full conversation with me. They earned my respect even more when they done that. They didn't care about no name, as they shouldn't. Then I started bickin it with the young homie Alwayz Active. Like he was put on by somebody in Hoboken New Jersey yet left stranded as well. Home girl 9 Lives from Van Ness Gangster Brims from the turf West South Central L.A....

We was also bick it everyday, telling me how fools use to come out there just to get some status and they own set. I'm like this shit beyond water down, the home girl Nine Lives ask when I'm coming to the turf. I'm like I'm trying to see now I get off papers early. I never had no dirty urine reports always ahead of time.

By this time I were seeing my federal probation officer every 3 months. I got out January 2014, it's about June 2015. I get a call from my first relative Trey, tells me about his son. On how he's dressing and that he was born and raised in Chicago. He feared his son was going in the gang path.

So one day Trey pulls up with his son, we sat at a restaurant but I asked Trey to step outside though. I call him my nephew, I'm like you really think it's cool to be dressing like a gang member huh....

You know anybody could dress like one, if you aren't putting in work daily it just a costume. I said matter of fact let me show you something. Then I ask him do you mind if I show you, his reply was yeah. At the time I believed he was 13, I lift up my shirt. I showed him my stomach first, you could see my scar it's what you call a zipper from right under my chest pass my nable. I told him I had 56 Staples, then lift up the shirt on my left side. Where you can see the knife went through all seven my ribs. Stomach wound from a bullet just missed the artery. Then I show him another scar, right under my left arm bullet pass my heart. Another stab wound where I bend my right arm at. Then finally the right side of my face, some five Deuce Hoover Crips graze me the right side of my temple. No rapper, nobody in prison out here in these streets could tell me about nothing. I experienced all of this by the time I was 16. Then I let him see my scroll tattoo scroll, from my left shoulder to where my arm bend at. A list of names of dead homies, that's from Jersey City in Newark.

At this time anybody that were dying and riding for this Brim shit that's where it was at included Paterson. Everybody else didn't do nothing in the beginning. Everybody else came after, far as in Jersey yet you got to include the whole Essex County. Anybody else that's representing Westside brim set. They all Millennium Bloods man this social media shit. Told my nephew straight up, next time your father Trey inform me you dressing like a gang banger.

We going to hop in the car we going to take a trip, going to be sober grab this bandana and this gun. You want to dress like one, you want to be one so you got to put in work. This what comes with gang banging gang life homie, this not no rap song no video game no nothing. All these names on my body, all these tombstones on me they die behind this shit. You can find out what Trey had to say and what nephew look like in "Invincible Tears Vol 1....

I'm finally off parole early, instead of doing the whole 3 years only did 19 months. That's a huge accomplishment because most done violated two or three times in a new charge. Truthfully I just didn't hang out 24/7 and most importantly I never once hit the block. I stay to my 9-5 job. I get a call from Fly Ti one afternoon, Mama Bradford she done pass a week after I spent the weekend with her.

You see Fly Ti is the youngest brother of J Vito and Mama Bradford is they mother. She definitely knew when J Vito was gone I was riding. That weekend she loved wearing my brim hat. Back to the conversation with Fly Ti though.

He like blood I'm going out to hood day and you deserve to come out here with me. All these other fools going out there didn't do half the shit you did. My reply was I was just speaking to the homie Dollarz about that, going out to L.A now that I'm off papers.

Fly Ti pay for part of my room, I paid for the ticket. Try to get the homie Killa to bum out there with me. By this time I'm already lacing everybody, different states and cities. I'm not asking nobody for no money no nothing. I'm literally only having like 15 dollars a week in my pocket. Constantly writing homies sending lot of pictures, it's so, at least 500 pictures in better. Sending them to multiple states and federal prisons.

I was writing HBo, Kaoss, Big Sha, Top Shelf, B G, Lock n Load, Killa E, Jawz Akbar Pray, No Exit, E Trillz, Killa Reek, Stacks, Big Pasha/Black and Mr. 187 host of other homies. Speaking of B G and Mr. 187 I received letters, from both of them right before I took flight 2 South Central L.A. B G letter was about touching on that four page letter I wrote him back and front. I'm the one talk blood out of going to trial, losing he would have got life. I told him I rather have him have lights at the end of the tunnel than none.

Don't do what a lot of these fools want you to do, next thing you know it he took his 35 years. Since I was out of prison, I was the only one checking on Mr. 187 family mama sister's son. Bought clothes sneakers all types, mind you by this time I was making like $9.50 an hour. Situation was I just care too much, that's all about to change though....

Separation Equals Growth

March 4th 2016 taking a flight to LAX. I was humble yet anxious to get out there, and by this time I'm the one that have the black n white on Vincent Young. It's one thing you can speak it, it's another when you have the actual paperwork. I'm on the plane I takeoff from this point forward, little did I know it take me to a whole new world in bracket. In our culture when, I land I meet up with Fly Ty and his brother. We go get the rental by time we get the rental, we double back L.A.X pick up a young homie from Charlotte North Carolina. Rented out apartment downtown L.A not too far from the Staples Center to be exact.

We was out there close to 14 days. I wasn't beat for nothing else it's time to hit the turf. We meet some homies at the Baldwin Hills Crenshaw Mall, then we pulled up to Budlong West South Central L.A. The first homies I met out there Lil Zee, Big Monster, Big Nino, MaKK 5, Rock Daddy, G Dogg and Killa MagiK. When I lock Brim with Killa MagiK, I tell blood I'm Gunna from Jersey City 36th Street.

Yeah we've been waiting to meet you, you rep ute able from out Jersey. He like do you know about the brims in New York the brims in the Carolinas the brims Virginia and started naming names. I'm like blood I didn't come out hear to bash other homies, all I can tell you none of these fools were Westside Brim before I went to prison. The only thing was back then was Fruit Town& Brick City Brim. Back then most was scared to be a West Coast set, right before I kept going I believe G Dogg was like blood take it to Lil Zee place.

Now as we following the G homies, me and Fly Ti. I get a call from Mr. 187, he in the feds now along with Gunz they were also lined up by the fool Los. I'm telling blood now we're about to head to one of the G homies houses. Mr.

187 like blood already know how you coming, you going to let these fools know. My response was on Brim Gang. We did too much shit behind this shit to let just go.

As we pull up we in the Eight Tray Gangster Crips section, this where Lil Zee was living at. As I step in the place it's about at least 40-something homies. That's when I met Tiny Jam, Lady 3rd the home girl, Baby Jam, Dirt in other's In I must say I felt very comfortable there, then we get right down to business. My response was, I don't know none of these fools, I can say they wasn't no Westside Brim anybody you name on the East Coast.

Back then you wasn't pushing no Van Ness Gangster Brims or Harvard Park Brims bottom line. When social media came out, that's when it was made easy for everyone to be in contact with you all. Like every time I turn around somebody got their own set that's pushing Harvard Park. This is a disgrace, I'm like my generation and generation before me we put in all Blood Sweat and Tears....

Then I pull out my phone started showing them homies that was locked up behind this Brim Gang. (The Names Were) Tweak, B G, HBo, Killa E, Hollow Tip, E Trillz, Mr. 187, Gunz, Big Dee, Big Pasha, Lock n Load, No Exit, Kaoss, Big Sha & Killa Reek and a host of others. They were calling Killa Reek, Lil Killa I'm like nah his name Killa Reek homie. I showed them a picture with me and Albee Al with the FHN hat.

They were so stuck on the hat they didn't even realize that was me in the picture. So they ask, who blood in the picture with the FHN hat I'm like that's me blood. The room just got quiet, they like damn blood you got on FHN hat on. I'm like blood I came out here for the dead homies that's on my body, homies that's locked up behind this shit. I done beat two hot ones, did 11 years behind this shit got kicked out my state. All I came out here for the truth, I don't be on the block all day, I don't hustle I don't do none of that I work.

March Maddmess 5678

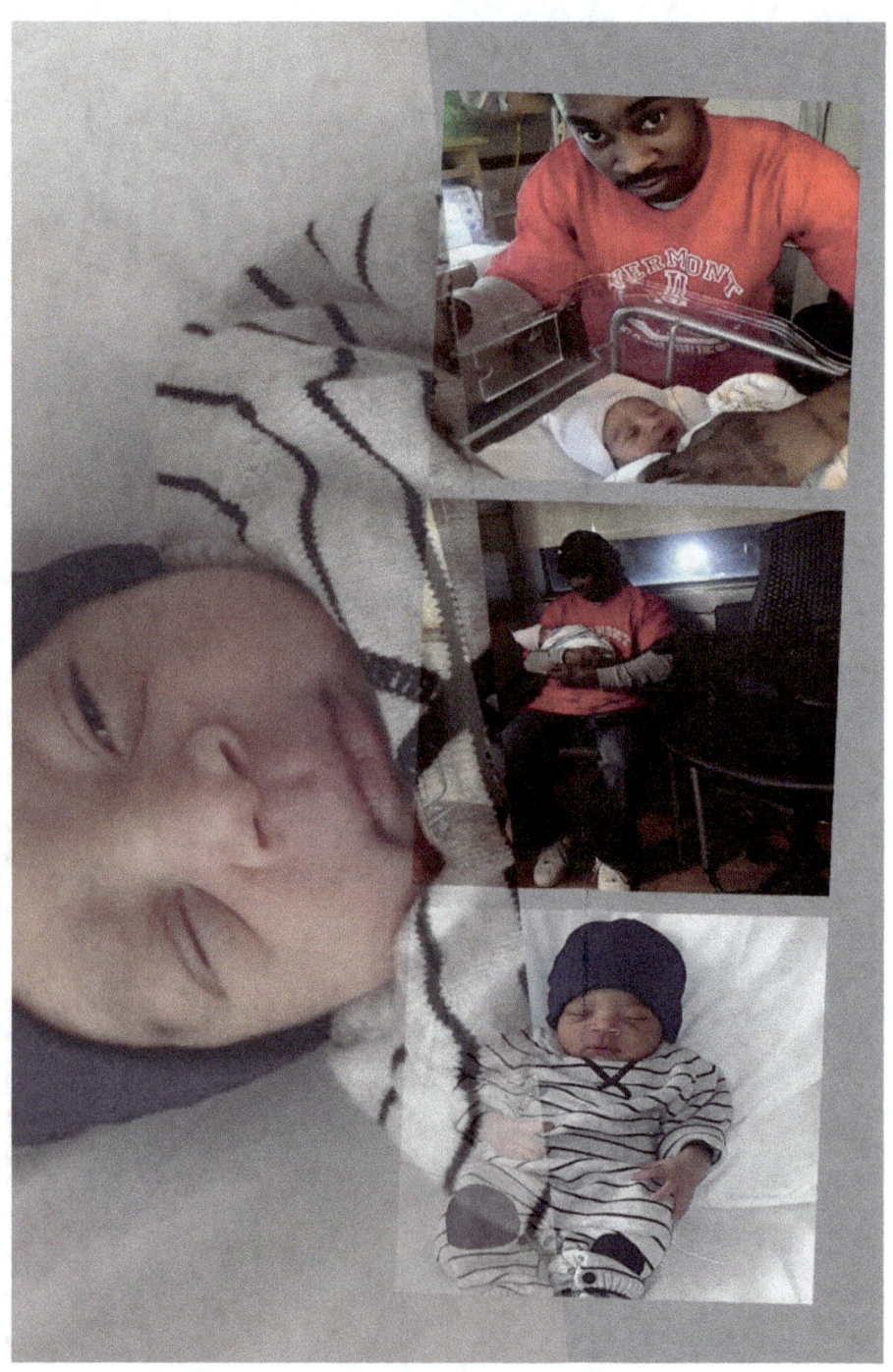

That's when on a dead homies, the G homies is like you start your own set Jersey North Carolina and Virginia. I'm like blood you're not listening, nobody can't give me nothing I'm already me. I came out here to know the history, do you know any of you how many homies we lost behind me sitting Jersey I don't care about no damn set. If that's why everybody flying out here, want to contact one of you for this so be it.

For me though by me knowing the truth, it means the homies that died for this shit didn't die for nothing. The homies that are doing ass hole full of time behind this isn't doing time for nothing. You all want me to take on this and turn around get the RICO conspiracy and all that I'm done with that shit. That's a little boy kid mentality, I'm a grown man with grown man responsibilities. We bick it for the rest of that night. Every homie embrace me that night, was surprised and respected my decision.

March 5th March Madness begins, Fruit Town Brim 35th Street it's they hood day. We special cause we the only set that have a hood week. Hood day is about the Dead and Gone, who paved the way. Celebrate those that still here in iron out hood politics that we needed iron out. It's our holiday. Now by this time we pick up YG then Dollarz, YG was a younger homie from Sanford North Carolina.

We was bickin it the whole time out South Central L.A Fly Ti pull up to a liquor store, blood not reading the walls no nothing. Just pulling up to anywhere. Him in another fool goes inside the liquor store. It's me YG and Dollarz, with the windows fully down. Small ass Essay walk up with a navy blue dickie suit all creased up, with the buckle hanging and navy blue chucks. I'm not going to lie to you blood, I watch his hands the whole time, essay like what's up homes where you from homies I have the full red bandana sweater with the brown brim hat on. YG have on all red and Dollarz have on the same sweater as me.

The essay got a long-ass extended clip hanging out his right pocket with his right hand on it. I'm just staring at his hand, Dollarz like we from Jersey in North Carolina. I'm saying in my head blood talking about what set we from. Of course he knew we were bloods, his reply was. If you were Crips, I would have smoked every last one of you. In went back somewhere down the alley in the dark. Blood when I say I was pissed I was pissed. I got on Fly Ti ass so fast, just pulling up to anywhere.

We headed to Bompton that's where the hood day function were at. When I stepped in their greeted the homies, the G homies immediately snatch me up. Took me to meet the founders of Fruit Town Pirus OGs from Neighborhood 20 Bloods this the night I actually met 9 Lives from Van Ness Gangster Brims and the home girl Lil Bitt from the Doves she from 27 block. In Bity Stone Bloods, Jungle Stone Bloods & Black P Stone Bloods met the homie Willie Brim from Harvard Park Brims host of others from Van Ness....

Later I was introduced to Big Kay-Bee then met Melly Mel. That's when I learned about Fruit Fridays every Friday is a Fruit Friday it's holiday. For everyone to get together. Amongst other things that don't need to be discussed. Now this when we found out Vincent Young was a Rollin 60 Crip first he didn't get put on in 88-89. Lied about Melly Mel, Ken Dogg, Ekuador even had us thinking D-Day and Rainbow got killed by some Crips. All this shit we were doing all this shit, come to find out hat boys is a Crip thang. Eastside Hat Gang Watts Crips no Brims go by hats.

From that night forward I said I'm always coming out here. Laid of opportunities and it didn't involve being in no gang. Now headed back to Virginia now all of sudden, I get so many friend requests. Like blood I haven't change who I was, I went out there as me I came back as me. Months later I get a phone call by Killa it's like 4 something in the morning. I knew it couldn't be bool, he like Spazz got killed. Immediately a tear came out my left eye, have to understand I watched him literally grow up. My reply was do you know who did it, he was like I'm trying to find out. I'm not even up there, I'm out Florida with my family and son.

When I get out there, this the first time any of these homies, seen me on some other shit. I'm remember I asked the homie for his address, blood broke down and cried on my shoulder talking about I can't give it to you. When I did finally get his address, I waited between 5 to 6 hours. Dedicated determined motivated, going back and forth with another homie. Who going to get the first shot off, I'm like blood whoever pull up everybody in that car everybody getting smoke....

Somebody in the inside which was the homies told blood that I was waiting. Then the following night, I tell somebody around Stegman n Ocean to get the strap. Blood pretended he was riding then pulled a

Boys in the Hood scene. I can't make this shit up. I just walked off in a young homie like what happened with blood. I'm like blood faking, you still see blood like he looking for something back of his truck.

I spent the block in just missed his bitch ass head. Another young homie the following day had the drop on him. Somebody else claiming he a big homie OG, he were so scary he pretended he seen the police riding down the block. A young homie had the dropped on the person that killed Spazz. He tells the young homie the police coming.

Everybody claim they love Spazz most didn't love no Spazz. For one the person that did it literally live directly around the corner, from where Spazz is from Stegman. For 2 everyone screaming they love him on social media yet wasn't at his wake or funeral. Most of the so-called homies from the set and most of the dudes that watch him grow up from Ocean. Now his uncle Wu came home from prison now everybody want to be in his face.

From that point on, I change how I dealt with homies. Nobody else can't say nothing about what's going on. I get to that in a second, literally six months later the homie Meech get killed. He too was lined up and back door by some homies that he was with. I remember the homie was looking for a parking space, I done already hopped out the car.

On Bidwell between Wegman and Ocean already had this big ass 4 pound in my hand, two people on the block I'm like blood you two need to slide homie. Bust 2 cK looking for the fools that lined up the homie. I'm from a whole different era all that crying and posting on social media. That's fake love just getting a bunch of likes and comments of somebody death. We in the time people be waiting for you to die, just to post a picture that they never posted before.

Months down the line I went back out to L.A this time I went by myself. The homie Smooth from Newport News Virginia. He went out to L.A meet me cause he knew, he meet the older generations that put banging into gang bangin. Big Kay- Bee threw me a stripper party and "Baldwin Village The Jays" the home of the Bity Stones Jungle Stones in Black P Stone Bloods. We were on Nicollet, for those that don't know, in the beginning they last name weren't Bloods it was Brims.

This the night I met the home girl from Bix Deuce Harvard Park Brims Baby Deuce and I also met Little John Jr. By this time is the second time I met the homie Uvg Trey, the function at his place. I liked blood he was laid back, he was into other shit wasn't extra out. This time I was out there for a few days.

While I was out there I met the homie Oyg Redrum 781 we was at Rancho Park. The same park 18th Street be at, that day it was all Bloods though. Athens Park Bloods, Neighborhood 20 Bloods, Campanella Park Piru, 104 Crenshaw Mafia Bloods, Jungle Stone Bloods, Black P Stone Bloods, Pasadena Denver Lanes, Fruit Town Brims host of other sets. I was there for my interview to be on Oyg Redrum documentary Blood Transfusion.

The home girl Lil Bitt was there, by this time she done healed up from her bullet wound. You know countless on the east coast is thinking it's fun in games out L.A thinking it's one big party. Not even knowing all Hood functions especially hood days somebody getting shot or killed. L.A has the most people in wheelchairs, that night March 5th 2016 Lil Bitt was shot in the back that night, ten others in 2 ended up dead.

Same night some home girls left another home girl, laid out on the ground shot. Fly Ti being a driver Dollarz keeping her calm, Y G holding her upper body rocking back and forth so she won't panic and I'm concealing her bullet wound keeping pressure on her wound. We driving all through Compton to find a certain Hospital. Because every hospital out their is for certain purpose.

We finally found one and me YG carried her in the hospital. Luckily she made it. I remember I told G Nutt my plans what I plan to do with the youth. I know as of now it seems like I'm never going to get there. By this time I'm having a son, I really can't believe I was having a son. By this time I'm making $14.50 an hour old trust me I'm still working. I just know how to save and put my needs first before my wants. A few nights before my son is born, the homie Fruit Town Fresh. It's me him and Maniak walking from the liquor store.

So Fruit Town Fresh like a woman by the name Lisa Chowdhury contacted him, and asked him if he mine going to speaking to the youth. The name of her organization is called Reimagining Justice out Paterson New Jersey. He said he told her he wasn't ready for that, he still out there slanging and gang banging. He told me he brought my name up immediately.

Like I have the perfect person for you. So he gave me her Gmail, he like you make sure you contact her because she going to be waiting. Honestly I was shocked that he gave me an information like that. I've been around all types of homies, they all kept claiming they was going to make it happen with somebody I can connect with.

I spoke about it all the time, that's what I really wanted to do. It was homies around me that have family members that were working with the youth. Working with Alternative kids all they kept doing was giving run around. I would never bring it up though, it is why to this day I don't deal with them. Like four nights later he on my heels, did you hit her yet, I'm like no.

Blood you wasting time what you waiting for. Hear comes Maniak Maine this all you talk about in prison man this is your chance. You be speaking shit these kids need to hear. That night I sent a nice bio about me to Lisa Chowdhury at her Gmail.

Surprisingly she hit me right back a few hours later. She loved what I had to say, then she did a three-way with Jason Davis. He loved our conversation then he asked me about status what I had. I believe all organizations they believe by a person having a certain status, it will reach kids when that is not the case.

Kids just want to know the truth, they are the most innocent creatures. They can sense when they are being lied to. I'm like I'm original homie. I'm one of the first come out my way. Nobody can't give me nothing. We set up to meet at Rutgers University in Newark at the hall. I'm not going to lie I was strapped, Crips like playing in that area a lot.

When I met Jason Davis and Lisa Chowdhury for the first time they were all smiles. In so was I. I brought a pro folio with me, things I had typed up before leaving prison my plans. They both was amazed that, I had this planned since being in prison. I inform both of them my own city, kept shutting me down.

They kept giving me the runaround. Long story short we setup to do something in the future. This time I'm they're my son is being born. I was beyond excited cause I still can't believe I was having a son. Truthfully my sisters and mama was more excited than me though. They all talking about if it's another girl leave her at the hospital laughs.

The very next month I get a call from both of them. Jason and Lisa on a three- way, would I like to educate alternative class in Newark. Hillside High they were seniors, speaking with the young men about respecting young ladies. How would they feel somebody disrespect they mama, sister, niece and cousin. So the same way you wouldn't like it, someone disrespecting your mama, relative, niece so on. You don't do it then, it's a two-way street.

Speaking to the young lady's about how they should dress. If you wear nothing you going to get treated like nothing. Not all young ladies in all woman looks for attention. Most dress the way they dress for attention, if you carry yourself with respect. Then you would definitely will receive respect, it is not always the case.

Some men are actually grown boys, but it's all up to you having standards about yourself. No one can take that away from you but you. You young men if you want respect you have to respect yourself first. Look how you dress, if you had a daughter she brought a young man to your house. Wants to be with her yet his behind hanging out will you respect him as a man let alone call him your son one day.

When he don't respect himself. Everything and anything in life starts with you first. After that we went to Rutgers University College. To teach a "Criminal Justice Class" I spoke on this on "Invincible Tears" Vol 1 I will say this though. Jason Davis touch on the word status of bloods. In I mention to him there's no such thing a West Coast blood sets status.

That just another way to control people. If I give you something, then I could take it right? how many times you heard a homie didn't do something. What that person did, downgraded they status or took it. It's a joke homies is paying for status oh if I send such in such money such in such. That's not how this Damu thing go.

Look at it this way to it's you, you give out four of the same status. That's already divide in concur, first thing somebody going to say I don't have to listen to you not my big homie. It always start like that I watch for decades go like that. If you take status away the numbers would definitely decline. Because they don't have nothing to take from this.

Show me one person that got put on for value of family, just one. You can't. Go any State City Coast there's no Unity nowhere. Either people from the East Coast buying a set on the West Coast they letting rappers pay to be a blood. Everyone out here bosses though.

Out L.A in Compton always speaking on out of towners yet they've been selling the B in the P from day one. In the music industry everyone situation is worrying about everybody else backyard but they own. 2 months later my sister Riri get me at my old high school Henry Snyder. Where I was a Credible Advocate from Freshmen to Seniors. I received a certificate and standing ovation that day.

Then I met Asheenia Johnson she invited me to come with her to Elizabeth at City Hall. Where, I public speaking about putting the guns down and education while young teenage gang members were there. The homie Dollarz in Smooth pulled up from Virginia to celebrate my birthday weekend. Had a birthday bash out in New York, Manhattan along with Ant from Armstrong Park he the man that made it happen that night put me on that list. When I was at work one day in the summer time.

I was getting so many missing calls but I always keep my phone on low volume. When I get off I get hit with a blow. My sister Lakeisha fell into a brain coma. On July 4th 2018 that Friday she asked to have her nephew Ausar my son for a week. She had a week vacation she wanted to spend time with him and of course I said yes.

By this time T Rogers reach out to me, say he love what I'm doing he want to work with me. For those that don't know, co-founder of Black P Stone Bloods T Rodgers Baldwin Village. Months later I step out with some fools one night. The same night I checked a snitch, for trying to give me peace. I told blood I catch him back when I'm sober.

People try to downgrade it yet forget. They were the ones that told me he snitched in the first place. That was a sign to leave them alone right then and there. We goes to a bar, a acting paranoid but drunk. He kept worrying about somebody just keep moving around. Keep in mind, I'm on him the whole time specially his hand. Yet he don't pose no threat he not looking our direction know nothing. Blood still goes over their in they section anyway.

He barking the next thing he got stole on, it's me in a Sex Money Murder homie beside me. We both stole on blood, still popping him then I had this it's not a shake. It has pocket knife a butter knife can opener all type of shit on their. Me seeing this fool fall I'm thinking I poked him up. Because I'm jigging it a few times in his back. It's very crowded in the back and inside.

So, I decide to leave out to get rid of it by the cemetery across the street. Once I throw it away and turn around. It's a homie that's outside he gets stole on and got dropped. I immediately run across the street where they at. I help pick blood up by that time the person that got stole on in the back of the bar. Was outside in the front squaring up with ol boy that dropped the homie.

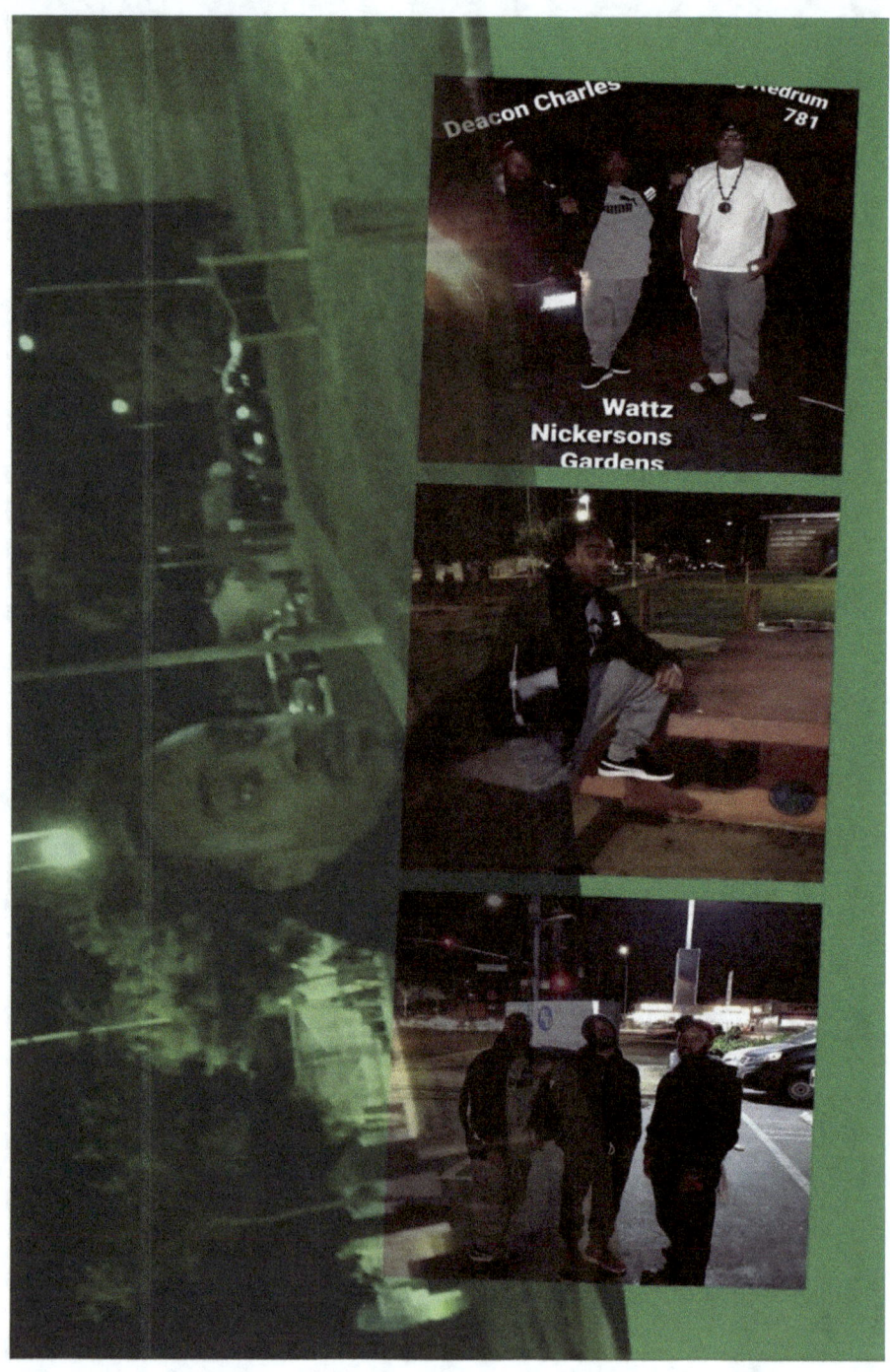

Once I help the homie that get dropped in the car. I follow suit side by side by the homie that got stole on. He's swinging with his head looking down, the homie that got stole on. Yet the person that drop the homie, he's never swinging he just keep backing up, keep backing up, keep backing up. Blood so drunk he don't even see what is behind ol boy.

I'm telling blood like back up you see that crowd back the fuck up. Next thing you know it shots ring out, I ducked in time. The shots were so close, I thought he got shot up. I'm screaming his name I'm screaming his name, luckily he just got shot in the leg. The whole time I'm saying in my head. I'm tearing everybody ass up for this one. Keep in mind I stood by his side the whole time.

The ambulance came and left, Drake from Armstrong Park and Hammer from Stegman n Jackson told me from the rip where they be at. First person I contact was his sister through Instagram. Let her know what hospital he was at and everything. Then I call Killa, Killa call another homie in then they came and snatched me up.

I had them drive by where them fools be at, before we even went down to the hospital. Went down to the hospital we found out everything was bool. The very next day I go up to Fulton & Bergen. Everybody just talking saying what they going to do what they would have did if they were their.

Nobody gave no dirt naps though. The person that got stolen on he outside as well. We hop in the car he drove me to Myrtle Ave, I'm like blood we should go around where 103 Rd Grape St Gangster Crips be at real quick. He like man I'm just going to wait. I'm like on dead homies, I just need you to be the driver that's it. On Spazz and J Vito blood, blood going to say he going to chill with his girl in the house.

I just got out the car and close the door talking about blood I love you. On my kids last breath from that night forward. I was done with him that's what I said in my mind. Right after that, I got picked up by some other fools. Me, Alwayz Aktive, Big D and Killa, I let them know I was there. It was a few other people there, I even mentioned that night I believe I poke a person up.

In Loving Memory Of Spazz

Fast forward a few days later, I get a phone call from a homie like the homie said you ran blood. The person that got stolen on, said someone told him that. Yet the person that told him that claim he fucks with but he didn't help him. I immediately called the fool that got stolen on. If I ran why you ducking my calls three times, for anything I'll be coming to see you if I knew you ran on me. Right after that I was outside that weekend because I don't live in Jersey.

From that point forward I was out with in Jersey City every weekend. Nobody said nothing to me nobody .... One night me and a fool we at a bar, my B day weekend. Took a couple of shots, this the same night I'm bickin it with the fool Tiny Wrench from Harvard Park Brims. He from the West South Central L.A updating me about some buster from Richmond Virginia.

We go down to the projects, keep in mind I decided to go down there on my own. Nobody asked me to go down there and I got a strap-on. The homie like yo you got to get DP blood. Let me bring it back though laughs. It was another homie that seen me he was on some scary shit. Because he the one whisper to the homie that had him say something to me.

I was bent but I was always on point. So back to the DP part, like I'm not getting DP blood there isn't no running in me. I said I'm the one that poked someone up how the fuck I ran. That's when it came out like there wasn't nobody that have get poked up. Being that I said I poke somebody, I took the DP nobody didn't make me do nothing. In I still didn't have to take no DP cause I've never ran. If I was scared to get jump why didn't I run from a DP.

I didn't have no scars no nothing in my DP. I was outside the very next day on Clinton. The person that got stolen on. Homies on Clinton told him I was around there he left and never came back. So let's see I had a strap on me that night I got DP. After the DP somebody else asked another homie why he didn't come down there.

Why nobody else came down there, his reply was they scared of Gunna. The person that said it was scared to look me in my eyes his damn self. Back to being around Clinton with no scars no bruises no nothing the next day after the DP. I told Always Aktive in Fruit Town Fresh about the DP they two was looking like where was the DP at. Fruit Town Fresh exact words was, I'm just waiting for who going to approach Gunna.

Nobody did I was outside the whole time. This the same night I found out that a homie pulled out on another homie because he disses his favorite rapper. Also I had a chance to finally see Stunna face to face. Because homies was going around saying he's the one that told ol boy that I was waiting for him. The whole time make sure we lock eyes to see he was stuttering lying anything I was going to do it right then and there.

Behind Spazz you damn right.... I never let that shit go. Once we got that straightened out he told me personally everybody screaming free him free him. All the people that's out there and they only put $40 for commissary. He said it loud in cleared for everybody to hear him and smutting his name. That man was damn near feeding everyone fools did him like that. Stunna exact words was, I remember when you Top Shelf and Killa E.

It doesn't matter how down you is what you did for people or nothing. Once you get behind them walls you forgotten. From that point on, that was my blessing to leave everybody alone. Ever since then I've been blessed. 2019 of August I was offered a job making $30 an hour working with alternative teenagers. Mob Piru homie out Newark had his own organization.

He got caught selling dope out of it. So that cancel everything the mayor wasn't dealing with nobody that had a record. I remember how excited I was informing certain individuals about working at all the Alternative Schools throughout Newark New Jersey for $30 an hour. That's not a job for something I love doing. In the end of October I goes back out to L.A this time I'm out there for 3 weeks. Killa MagiK introduced me to his family wife and kids.

This time I'm staying at the homie Uvg Trey place. Oyg Kre Kre and Mama Boo from Athens Park Bloods pulls up while I'm at Uvg Trey place. Oyg Kre Kre has two books out Piru Love part 1 & 2. I bang Oyg Redrum line and I pulled up in the Nickerson Gardens Projects in Watts,

California. That's where Oyg Redrum 781 were living at. Introduce me a couple of the Bounty Hunter homies, I spent the whole day and night down there just bickin it and I also met most of his kids.

So the g homie pick me up Deacon Charles he's also author "Let Me Tell You How I Got Saved" we outside blood door down the projects. You heard so much artillery let off down and Gardens. Like it's time to go laughs. We stopped at a soul food place, then I ran into Barefoot Pookie the co-founder of Westside Crips. Also the founder of Gardena Paybacc Gangster Crips.

His wife complimented my locks, then we all started talking about the strength what it represents. By this time I started introducing everybody by my real name. I like Barefoot Pookie no what, I do with the youth and young teenagers. We both definitely agree the generations behind us need to do better. Deacon Charles and his son stood off to the side.

I shook Barefoot Pookie hand and his wife, then he gave me his home phone number. Not too long after that we headed to Harvard Park, me the deacon and his son. Just building in reminiscing, then we pulled up to Lawndale. Me and Uvg Trey went out to this spot out in Gardena. Nice chill little spot. The next day though Big Kay-Bee and G-Shock pulls up on me.

This when I gave Big Kay-Bee a new picture of me and my son, so he took the old one out his wallet and put in the new one. G-Shock like we finally met blood. He said he been wanted to meet me. G- Shock, Big Kay-Bee and me just reminiscing. That very same night Big Teddy Bear and Lil A Dogg from Neighborhood 20 Bloods the home girls.

You see Neighborhood Bloods got our front we got they back. It's 20 Fruits they pick me up take me to they turf West Adams. I meet up with the home girl Tay Tay and Big Jimbo. I came across Melly Mel and the homie Hunter from 36th Street Fruit Town Brims. Melly Mel remember me from hood day, he said to me I know you a brim your walk.

I'm just receiving game wisdom just listening. I was the youngest out there that night. There was only second third generation. Big Teddy Bear Lil A Dogg and me we going to the Outlaws 20 Bloods. This where I met Jay Rock and Top Dogg, were coming out of the Outlaws 20s liquor store. They both Deuce Line from Bounty Hunter Bloods, Top Dogg started top dawg entertainment. Very few days later I'm met the homie from Holly Hood Piru Bad Seed he's from Bompton.

He like blood I be following you on the grams you be speaking some solid shit. I take a flight back home. Very few days later, Big Jimbo was killed. I'm like damn I was literally just over there speaking to him. Second generation of the Doves. After that I found a sister I never met before and a brother. Sad part I lost a brother that same day I found him.

He already done passed from stage 4 cancer. He didn't even know he had siblings full of nieces and nephews. His name is Samuel Jr. I found them both the day after my son birthday party off Facebook. On January 29th 2020 Lisa Jason inform me on some great news. That they were given a grant for 29 million dollars, so they call me about salary.

Lisa asked me $45,000 was cool with me. I said that's great that's better when I'm getting. I don't look at it as a job anyway, it's my passion. So the paper work everything supposed to been finalized by the end of April. Covid happening March and it seemed it was like, I wasn't never going to accomplish my dream.

Then Lord gave me a sign, it's time for you to pack up and go if you want to reach another level. I haven't left yet I was still debating, started enjoying myself more traveling to other places. Treating myself to Ocean City Maryland for my birthday. Following month went out to ATL pulled up on Juelz first time either one of us seeing each other face-to-face.

Since being out of prison, took him in a Fruit Town Brick City Brim homie Twist from Newark to meet Rock Daddy. That's when Rock Daddy told Twist and Juelz. The reason why him the homies fuck with me so much. I was just mem, I didn't come out there looking for nothing begging for nothing. That following week, I flew out back to L.A met Big Lunatik the home girl from OutLaw 20 Bloods.

I remember one night me Big Lunatik and Uvg Trey coming from down Hollywood yet stopped in the Fruit Town Brims. Leaving from there the cops way on the other side. Going to try in say the home girl was on her phone. She wasn't never on her phone they were just racist. They pulled us over in a Rollin 60 neighborhood. I'm thinking we straight this shit going in and out. Check the license plates all that we out of here.

The whole time, I'm calm as a fan as I should. L.A laws is very very different, when it comes to gangs. Keep in mind we got pulled over in the Rollin 60's Crips hood. The exact same spot and Boys in the Hood the movie. The scene when they get harassed by the police.

Mind you I have gang tats Rollin 60s whacked out Rollin 40s and Harlem 30 Crips all wacked out on my body. In my mind I'm like, just for having gang tat is 10 years another ten years to be in possession of a gun as a gang member. Another 10 years getting caught in the enemy set saying that you was going to commit some killings.

That's automatic 30 years without the actually charge. They found her strap the home girl, Big Lunatik she took it like a g. I made sure her father get her belongings. I flew back home. Then months later that I flew back out to ATL that's when I met Erica Gardner the home girl from 9 Deuce Bishop Bloods she's originally from L.A then I flew out to Pasadena Texas.

Relax with my relatives Trey for a couple of days before I head back home. I was on vacation from my job, I was working for Jews so you know they have their own holidays and days off. By the of 2020 Akbar Pray wrote me a letter. Also a play, after I had sent him pictures of what I was doing with the youth and teenagers.

He wrote me a play called Death Of The Game. The same title is title of his book, as well Last Of A Dying Breed. Which he be giving me 20 copies of that, I was supposed to fly out to L.A the beginning of March. Something told me to cancel my round trip, on March 6th I was supposed to meet a young homie from North Philly. His name was Tay his set was Elm Street Piru he got killed out Bompton the same night we were supposed to have meet up. Already met him prior out North Philly, by Oyg Kre Kre.

Oyg Kre Kre he was shooting his documentary for "World Wide Woopin". Same day I had to check a person, all because he tried to perpetrate an image. Going to try to tell me in Oyg Kre Kre the way we piece Brim is wrong. Then took it further, the way he said he try to piece he does that out in turf.

When he felt embarrass, he going to say he a big homie he Og laughs. I'm like no you not I'm original and I'm not from Philly homie I'm from Jersey. I'm one of the main many reasons you throwing up Brim. April 1st 2021 that's when everything really changed for my life. I invested in myself and I never looked back again the end....

A Messages to My Readers

May everyone that read my story, felt motivated and inspired. To see that I never gave up, everything that was thrown at me literally everything. I still kept the faith, my story I just wanted to drop some jewels. Especially for the youth and young teens. Show you the seriousness, that come from gang banging and snitching as well hanging with one. For example it was another person that made a statement on B G and Killa E.

At the time, I didn't have the black and white. Being that he said something to homicide, Gunz punch him in his shit twice. Then I grab him pistol-whipping him three times in his jaw broke in two places. Then when I did get the paperwork, it was me Dead Wrong, Gunz, Mr. 187, No Exit, Fly Ti , Rah, Manika Maine walk to Bostwick n Jackson.

I lead the charge going to his house, he ran inside some apartment building everyone said, Gunna he gone you isn't going catch him. I say this to say he knew what he did, soon he seen my face he ran. Yet I spent so much time wasted, I had auntie named Maryanne that passed. My mama oldest sister, I'm so caught up trying to find the truth.

Make sure the streets right, in the homies behind the wall right. She passed in her sleep about three years I was already home. I never took the time to go see her once, since I've been out of prison. You know the last time I seen my auntie.

Right before I was arrested, me coming out the building on Stegman n Bergen. With my snub nose 38, as she seen the burner in my hand. She screaming know Julius know Julius don't do it. As I lift my hands I have the gun pointed on top of somebody head. My brother Tai Quwan stop me from pulling the trigger. He said I was bugging it was too many people outside. I spent my whole life sacrifice my life and freedom, for everyone that didn't give a damn about me.

Yet the key is, you have to give a damn about yourself before anybody else can. I didn't here from no homies while I was in prison. I still remained me I never went around bashing anybody. I knew what I signed up for, nobody don't owe me nothing but me. I owe myself everything and more. So many men are broken older men, it is why I force on these young teenagers.

The second I started investing in myself, everyone started distance themselves. Which was pretty much appreciated it, now I blossom to my full potential. I had got my LLC. For Envinsable Teirs LLC because I do gang intervention, prevention. Educational guidance, I deal with trauma depression. When I met a Asheenia Johnson we went to City Hall out Elizabeth New Jersey.

If she wouldn't have invited me that night, I would have never met a person who had his own sitcom to have my interview on TV and on YouTube. BASA TV interview close to a hour. It's on my website: envinsableteirs.blogspot.com

Then later on I met in May, community function for the community and kids. We back outside by Brandon Banks that started his career in "NFL" Washington Redskins now plays for the "CFL" and Emanuel Davis started his career in "NFL" Cleveland Browns now retired from "CFL" after winning a grey bowl in "2020". I had signed up for College online Colorado University my major Criminal Justice Social Science I was given 4.0. Fortunately I had to stop make sacrifice. Lack of support yet I still kept my vision. Even started working on a counsel at Norfolk State University Educational Industries Building.

My website going to be the headline for it, alongside with Temond Jones. It's going be about teaching economics, rape, gangs, incarceration, brutality, needs and wants, bridging the gap between men and women relationships....

Then I was invited to a community event out Compton California. In the Campanella Park Pirus they were given they community book bags full of school supplies and high jeans. I was invited by Og Tray Bo and his wife Tye Girl. I was introduced Og Tray Bo by his little sister Lillian Davis. I spent three months in Los Angeles.

Just networking been on a couple of podcast. First by second generation Nino Cappuccino Rule OF Engagement. He from Nickerson Gardens Watts California. I did two interviews back to back on podcast called Sparks Fly. It's on Spotify an Apple season 2 "Bridging the gap to the youth and The history of the bloods on the east coast. Since I was in L.A I attended T Rogers funeral and wake. I attended it cause we had plans. To go State to State City to City speak to the youth inside the schools. Elementary High School in Colleges. By redirecting changing the narrative, cause these kids don't have no role models. Everyone out here especially grown men, just continue glorifying a genocide. Most haven't experience and lived.

There's nothing glorifying about it, 75% of my pictures they are all dead. Where is the humor in that, I have over 35 names on my body that are dead. Behind gang banging, yet I lost over 82 homies. By the time I was 17 I've been over 20 funerals. All due to gun violence. Rappers that be reppin these sets, most of them getting extorted. Trust me I know, I can put people favor rappers out there even the paperwork I have seen. Even some of your favorite DJs. In the feds it's so much paperwork on people it's ridiculous.

I left a lot of things out. It's about a message, I'm not here to bash anyone. I could have easily made part 2, I left a lot of names out in situations out so I won't get to bashing. As well I will be doing another book anyway about my life. I was even a part of a Blood and Crip peace treaty. Along with Oyg Redrum 781 and Jason Davis. I speak about in my first book "Invincible Tears Vol 1" a lot of other things I did in the community. It's all in volume one, you could also see pictures on the people I'm speaking on in volume one. I'm showing you and giving you first hand.

If you want to achieve anything in life, go to the next level in life. Watch and look out for the signs. Going to have to separate yourself, to elevate in life. The Lord and I repeat the Lord will not put you in the position to your full potential if you not surrounding yourself with like-minded people. In most importantly, if you not putting in the footwork and taking initially steps to achieve each goal you set out for yourself.

The plan is longevity not short-term yet long-term. Even though I go out to L.A all the time. I don't get no support from out there, besides OG Chucky Cheese, Big Kay-Bee and g homie Deacon Charles. Shout out to Big Nino for pulling up in Jersey looking for me yet I wasn't in town. In MaKK 5 for coming to Camden and Jersey City, New Jersey. REST PEACE TO EVERY FALLING....

In the Crips I was going at 5 Deuce Hoover Crips, Rollin 60 Crips I hope the readers get something from this much gratitude..

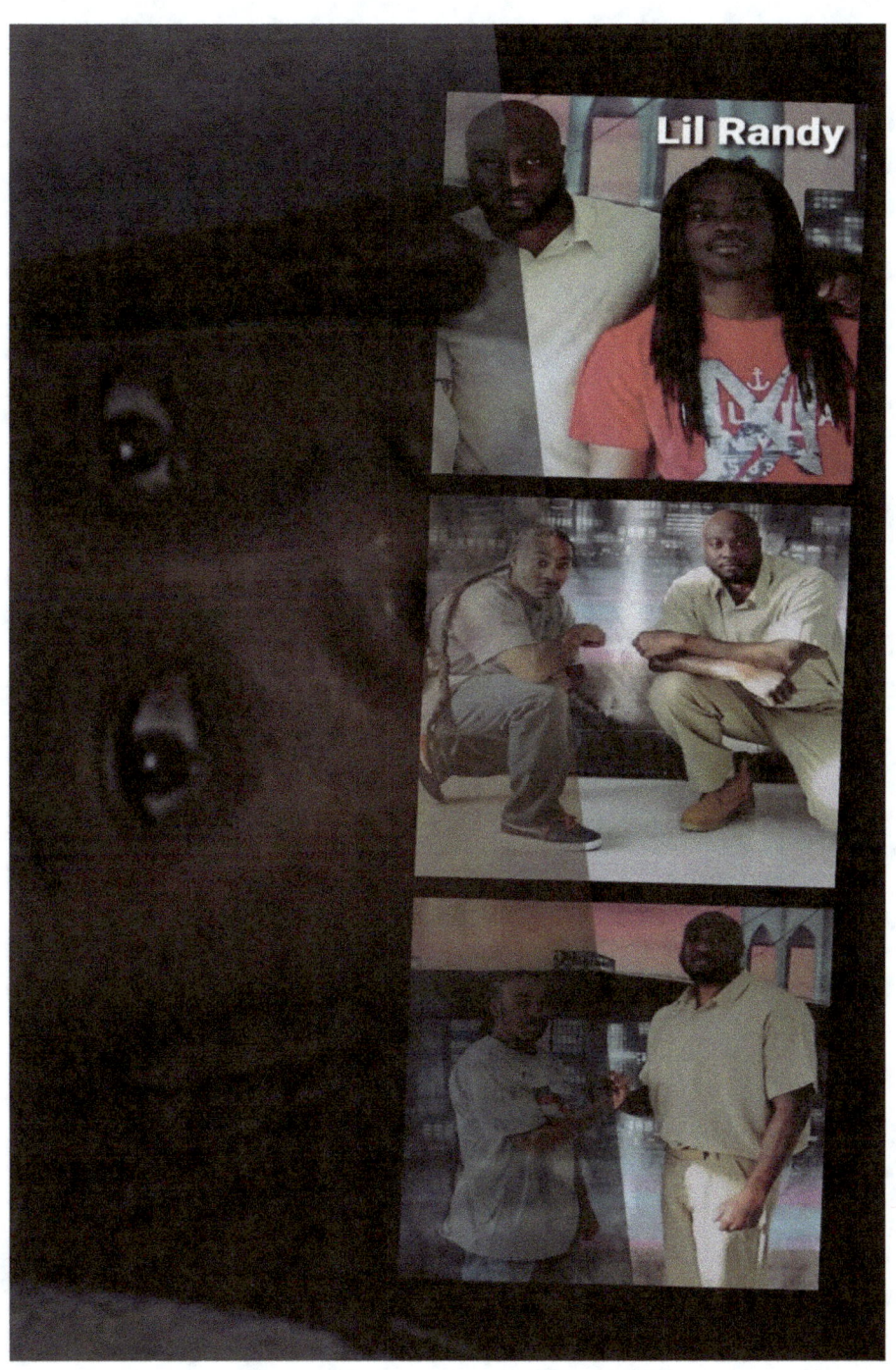

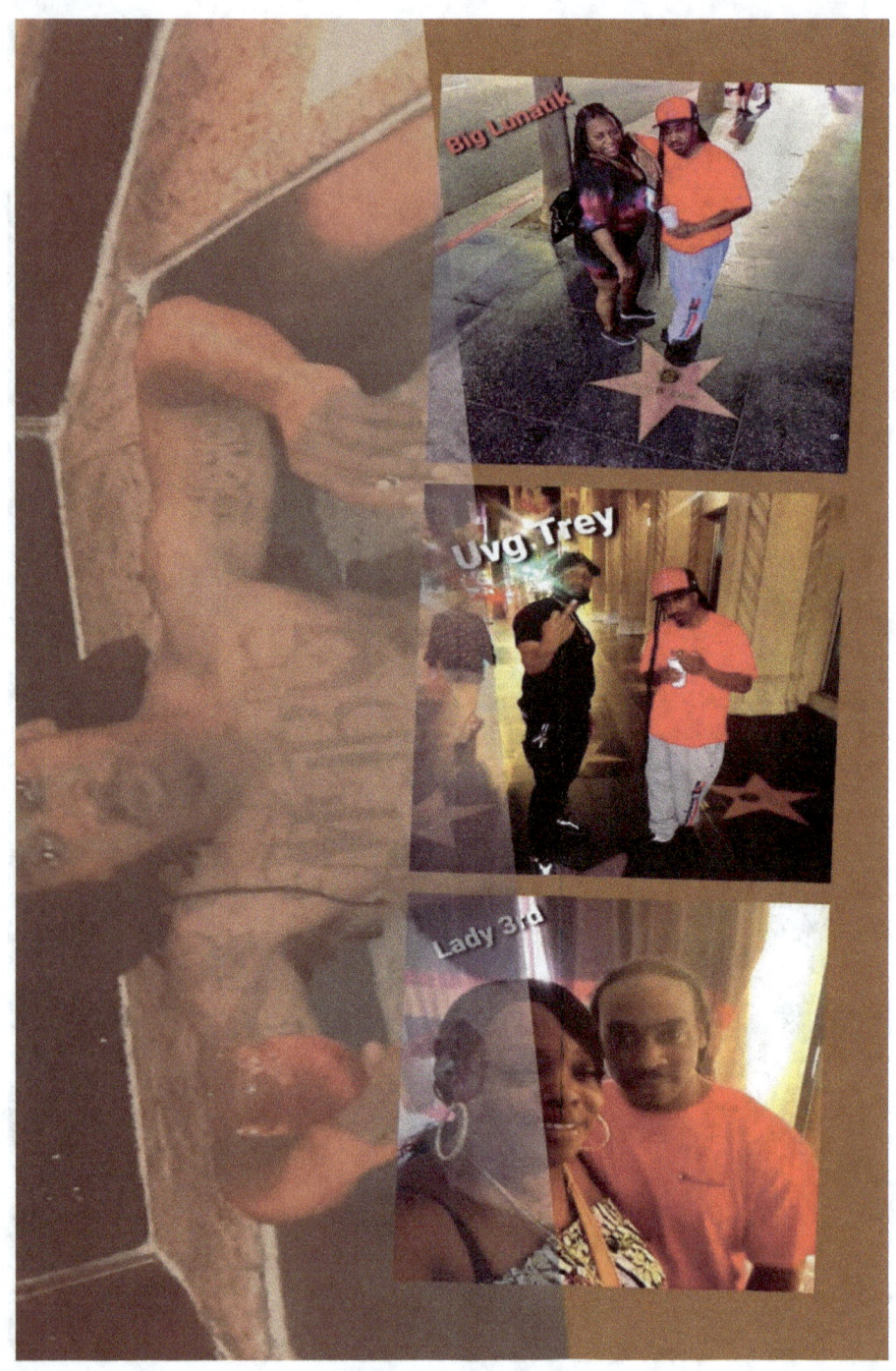

Specially Thanks

I lost everything believing in myself staying dedicated and motivated. In I couldn't do it without you "The Lord" nothing is impossible longs you in my life and bless me with this special gift.

Mama thank you for never turning up your nose up at me any time, I spoke about my plans. Trey you been on me about writing a book about my life since being out of prison here goes.

It were times, I felt like giving up just your simple messages kept me going the 3 month's I spent out L.A Jason Davis, Mama Maryann, Riri, Twin Twin and Mama Burks….

I'm looking forward to doing more Volumes and getting Crips involved as well more women.